# OLD TESTAMENT MESSAGE

*A Biblical-Theological Commentary*

Carroll Stuhlmueller, C.P. and Martin McNamara, M.S.C.

EDITORS

*Old Testament Message, Volume 19*

# SIRACH

R. A. F. MacKenzie, S.J.

Michael Glazier, Inc.
Wilmington, Delaware

First published in 1983 by: MICHAEL GLAZIER, INC. 1723 Delaware Avenue, Wilmington, Delaware 19806
Distributed outside U.S., Canada & Philippines by: GILL & MACMILLAN, LTD., Goldenbridge, Inchicore, Dublin 8 Ireland

Library of Congress Catalog Card Number: 82-83725
International Standard Book Number
  *Old Testament Message series:* 0-89453-235-9
  SIRACH
    0-89453-253-7 (Michael Glazier, Inc.)
    7171-1183-0 (Gill & MacMillan, Ltd.)

Cover design by Lillian Brulc
Typography by Susan Pickett
Printed in the United States of America

# CONTENTS

# Editors' Preface

*Old Testament Message* brings into our life and religion today the ancient word of God to Israel. This word, according to the book of the prophet Isaiah, had soaked the earth like "rain and snow coming gently down from heaven" and had returned to God fruitfully in all forms of human life (Isa 55:10). The authors of this series remain true to this ancient Israelite heritage and draw us into the home, the temple and the marketplace of God's chosen people. Although they rely upon the tools of modern scholarship to uncover the distant places and culture of the biblical world, yet they also refocus these insights in a language clear and understandable for any interested reader today. They enable us, even if this be our first acquaintance with the Old Testament, to become sister and brother, or at least good neighbor, to our religious ancestors. In this way we begin to hear God's word ever more forcefully in our own times and across our world, within our prayer and worship, in our secular needs and perplexing problems.

Because life is complex and our world includes, at times in a single large city, vastly different styles of living, we have much to learn from the Israelite Scriptures. The Old Testament spans forty-six biblical books and almost nineteen hundred years of life. It extends through desert, agricultural and urban ways of human existence. The literary style embraces a world of literature and human emotions. Its history began with Moses and the birth-pangs of a new people, it came of age politically and economically under David and Solomon, it reeled under the fiery threats of prophets like Amos and Jeremiah. The people despaired and yet were re-created with new hope during the Babylonian exile. Later reconstruction in the homeland and then the trauma of apocalyptic movements prepared for the revelation of "the mystery hidden for ages in God who created all things" (Eph 3:9).

While the Old Testament telescopes twelve to nineteen hundred years of human existence within the small country of Israel, any single moment of time today witnesses to the reenactment of this entire history across the wide expanse of planet earth. Each verse of the Old Testament is being relived somewhere in our world today. We need, therefore, the *entire* Old Testament and all twenty-three volumes of this new set, in order to be totally a "Bible person" within today's widely diverse society.

The subtitle of this series—"A Biblical-Theological Commentary"—clarifies what these twenty-three volumes intend to do.

Their *purpose* is theological: to feel the pulse of God's word for its *religious* impact and direction.

Their *method* is biblical: to establish the scriptural word firmly within the life and culture of ancient Israel.

Their *style* is commentary: not to explain verse by verse but to follow a presentation of the message that is easily understandable to any serious reader, even if this person is untrained in ancient history and biblical languages.

*Old Testament Message*—like its predecessor, *New Testament Message*—is aimed at the entire English-speaking world and so is a collaborative effort of an international team. The twenty-one contributors are women and men drawn from North America, Ireland, Britain and Australia. They are scholars who have published in scientific journals, but they have been chosen equally as well for their proven ability to communicate on a popular level. This twenty-three book set comes from Roman Catholic writers, yet, like the Bible itself, it reaches beyond interpretations restricted to an individual church and so enables men and women rooted in biblical faith to unite and so to appreciate their own traditions more fully and more adequately.

Most of all, through the word of God, we seek the blessedness and joy of those

who walk in the law of the Lord!...

who seek God with their whole heart (Ps. 119:1-2).

*Carroll Stuhlmueller, C.P.    Martin McNamara, M.S.C.*

# INTRODUCTION

The book of Sirach has had various titles in the course of its history. Originally known as "The Wisdom of Ben Sira" or "The Proverbs of Ben Sira," in its Latin version it was called *Liber Ecclesiasticus,* "the Church book," apparently because it was so popular as an aid to catechetics in the early centuries of the Western Church. It also had the distinction of being, next to the Psalter, the Old Testament book most frequently cited in the Roman liturgy. Unfortunately that title sometimes led to confusion with Ecclesiastes, a quite different work, and still more to confusion of the abbreviations, "Ecclus" and "Eccles" respectively. Here we shall refer only to "Ben Sira," of which "Sirach" is the Greek form.

## Date

Thanks to the Greek translator's Prologue (see below), the date of the work can be closely fixed, between 200 and 175 B.C. It may have been issued in two or even three successive volumes or instalments: besides the final conclusion 50:27-29, there are what look like two earlier conclusions, now in the middle of the book: 24:32-34; 33:16-18.

## Religious Background

Throughout the third century B.C. the Jews, both those inhabiting Judea and still more those in other areas, were living in a hellenized world. Since the conquests of Alexander the Great (died 323 B.C.) Greek culture had transformed the cities, and to some extent the countryside, of the whole Near East, including Egypt, Palestine, Syria, Babylonia and Persia. That culture included not only philosophy, literature, athletics, etc., but also the polytheistic religion of Greece. The latter obviously was quite irreconcilable with the strict traditional monotheism of the Hebrews. The Jews had the delicate problem of conforming themselves to "modern" standards of civilized living, while at the same time preserving in practice the essentials at least of their traditional monotheism, supported by the observances of the Mosaic Law. As long as Palestine remained subject to the Egyptian kings, the Ptolemies, ruling from Alexandria, the problem does not seem to have been felt as acute; provided Jerusalem paid its taxes, the Ptolemies left it alone. But when the province was transferred (about 200 B.C.) to the control of the Syrian kings, the Seleucids, ruling from Antioch, the tension between Hellenizers and Judaizers gradually but steadily increased, till it culminated in the Maccabean uprising, 166 B.C. It was by no means a simple case of external vs. internal pressure. Hellenism, with idolatry and paganism included, had many influential adherents among the Jews themselves, and the struggle was largely within the community. Ben Sira's work however reflects an early stage of the process, and though he bitterly reproaches the "apostates" (2:12-14; 41:8) for the most part he takes for granted that his hearers are as loyal and faithful to "the tradition of the fathers" as he is himself.

## Author

Although he took the trouble to sign his work (50:27), the full form of the author's name is not quite sure: most probably it was "Joshua ben Eleazar ben Sira" (the Greek equivalent of "Joshua" is "Jesus"; "ben" means "son of"). He was a citizen of Jerusalem, of a prominent and well-to-do family ("Sira" was apparently the name of his grandfather). He received a pious upbringing and a good education; probably he was trilingual, knowing Aramaic and Greek as well as Hebrew. From boyhood he was devoted to the pursuit of wisdom, i.e. the course of scribal instruction and the study of the sacred books. He traveled widely, and perhaps served under a gentile king. After his travels he settled in Jerusalem where he raised a family and maintained a large establishment. If not a merchant, he was at least familiar with business affairs. As an experienced and learned man he took his place in civic administration and among the judges. But above all, he was a sage and a pedagogue. The youths of the Jerusalem aristocracy were sent to him for instruction, and the poetic discourses which make up this long book were no doubt originally recited before his students and committed to memory by them.

## *Doctrine*

Ben Sira has no private axe to grind, no pet theory to develop, like Ecclesiastes or the author of Job. He aims at synthesizing and harmonizing a vast body of traditional material; more precisely, at combining into one consistent philosophy of life two originally quite distinct traditions, which already before him had begun to influence one another. These were, first, the Mosaic tradition of salvation-history, with its covenant-theology; second, the international Wisdom tradition of the ancient Near East, which when it touched on theology stressed rather the theology of Creation, and knew nothing of any special relationship of one particular nation to the Creator. The two traditions had already made contact in the book of Proverbs, where the unique Creator, who despatches the divine Wisdom down to earth to offer herself to humankind, is firmly identified with Yahweh, the God who established his covenant through Moses with Israel alone. The meaning and scope of the word "wisdom" leave it ambiguous, since it continued to be used on several different levels. Originally it meant no more than "skill," technology, the ability to adapt or control sectors of material reality, of the physical world, for the advantage of humankind. Thus, the hunter, the trapper, the farmer, the weaver, the potter, would each have his or her proper "wisdom," to be established by trial and error, then to be transmitted partly by example partly by verbalization to the next generation. But at a higher level the word was used of social relations, meaning tact or diplomacy, "how to win friends and influence people," and it is with that meaning that it is used in the older parts of the book of Proverbs. A third level higher still applied the word to the Creator himself: since Wisdom is so precious a thing, it follows that God must have his own, which will naturally be infinitely superior to any human wisdom and quite inaccessible to humankind — *unless* indeed (and here is a fourth "level") God in his goodness chooses to communicate it, by revelation, to (some of) his creatures. That is what he is shown as doing to humankind generally, in Prov 8; but Ben Sira goes one step further, and identifies the "revelation" with the covenant-making at Sinai. Thus this great gift of divine Wisdom turns out to have been, all along, in the possession of Israel: divine Wisdom = the Law of Moses. But this Law, for Ben Sira, is by no means the same concept as that of the later Pharisees and Rabbis; see below on 24:23.

Another important factor in Ben Sira's synthesis is an intense appreciation and defense of the cult, and of the role of priesthood in the Jewish community. This is new in wisdom writing—earlier sages felt that such material lay quite outside their competence. But Ben Sira saw the great importance, for the defense of Judaism, of attachment to the Temple ritual among the laity, and of conscientious leadership among the priests — though in fact, when the crisis came, the latter was sadly lacking.

Another concept which Ben Sira does much to clarify is that of the Canon: namely, a collection of sacred and authoritative writings containing an account of God's relations with mankind and with Israel. He systematically draws on this collection for his Bible history, the "praise of famous men"; see below on 44:1-49:16.

On another important subject, however, he has nothing new to say: the prospect of a judgment after death, and the possible separation of the good from the wicked in a future life. Abiding by the doctrine of Proverbs (and the rest of the then existing scriptures), he denies any such judgment or discrimination; death ends all, and the "ghosts" of virtuous and vicious alike descend to the Under World. His grandson-translator however did believe in a judgment, and once or twice has modified his translation to express this (e.g. 7:17).

Among the appealing characteristics of Ben Sira we may mention his doctrine on forgiveness of enemies (28:2-7), and his repeated denunciations of oppression of the poor and helpless (e.g. 34:18-22). Less attractive to modern readers may be what sounds like excessive severity in his recommended treatment of sons and daughters (30:1-13; 42:9-14), and his "male chauvinism" in discussing marriage. The latter consists not so much in his violent censure of the "evil wife" (he can be equally violent against his own sex), as in the male-centeredness of the whole discussion. He never canvasses what the "good husband" ought to be or do, from the woman's point of view. Similarly, he might have found many a "valiant woman" worthy to be mentioned in his Bible history; but that gallery is "for men only." We can only say that he was a man, speaking to men and living in a man's world. We cannot demand of him later sensibilities, such as those (for example) of St. Luke.

## *Canonicity*

Around the end of the first century A.D. the surviving Rabbis in the south of Palestine, mostly of the Pharisee party, discussed the closing of their Canon of Scripture: what should be the complete list of sacred books, not to be added to? For reasons we can only guess at, they excluded Ben Sira: possibly because written too recently, after the holy Spirit had departed from Israel; or possibly because it disagreed with the Pharisee doctrine of resurrection. On the other hand, as part of the Septuagint, which the early Church took over as its Old Testament, the book was automatically accepted by Christians, and made much use of for catechesis and in liturgical readings. From the Greek, a Latin translation was made (not by St. Jerome) and included in the Vulgate. Thus practically all Christians, east and west, held the book to be canonical for over 1000 years. It was not until the 16th century that the Reformers decided to adopt the restricted Hebrew canon, and put the "extra" books of the Greek and Latin Bibles in a separate category as "Apocrypha." The preferred Catholic label is "Deuterocanonica."

## Text

The original Hebrew text of the book, once it was refused a place in the Jewish canon, soon ceased to be copied, and dropped out of sight. In modern times about two thirds of it have been rediscovered, and can be used in modern translations. See RSV footnotes. The Greek translation (see the Prologue) was preserved by Christians, much used and much copied. In the process, the text was often expanded and added to, with glosses and insertions of all kinds. When the verse numeration was added (16th century A.D.) these additions were included in the numbering; but modern translations (e.g. RSV) mostly eliminate them. This explains why there are so often gaps in the verse numbering of the text: secondary additions to the text have been skipped, or put in RSV footnotes.

# THE PROLOGUE

1. Whereas many great teachings have been given to us through the law and the prophets and the others that followed them, on account of which we should praise Israel for instruction and wisdom; and since it is necessary not only that the readers themselves should acquire understanding but also that those who love learning should be able to help the outsiders by both speaking and writing, my grandfather Jesus, after devoting himself especially to the reading of the law and the prophets and the other books of our fathers, and after acquiring considerable proficiency in them, was himself also led to write something pertaining to instruction and wisdom, in order that, by becoming conversant with this also, those who love learning should make even greater progress in living according to the law.

3. When I came to Egypt in the thirty-eighth year of the reign of Euergetes and stayed for some time, I found opportunity for no little instruction. It seemed highly necessary that I should myself devote some pains and labor to the translation of the following book, using in that period of time great watchfulness and skill in order to complete and publish the book for those living abroad who wished to gain learning, being prepared in character to live according to the law.

2. You are urged therefore to read with good will and attention, and to be indulgent in cases where, despite our diligent labor in translating, we may seem to have rendered some phrases imperfectly. For what was originally expressed in Hebrew does not have exactly the same sense when translated into another language. Not only this work, but even the law itself, the prophecies, and the rest of the books differ not a little as originally expressed.

This prologue was written in Greek by the Greek translator and was not part of the original Hebrew work of Ben Sira. Hence it is not considered inspired and is not part of the canonical book. It is, however, a valuable historical document giving accurate and important information about the book and the author. It consists of three paragraphs, but in the traditional texts the second and third paragraphs have changed places. Our text restores the original order, ##1, 3, 2. The writer was Ben Sira's grandson, whose name we do not know. He was bilingual, that is, fluent in both Hebrew and Greek, though more at home with Greek, which he spoke every day. In the year 132 B.C. he emigrated from Palestine to Egypt, bringing with him a scroll containing his grandfather's wisdom writings. In Egypt, probably at Alexandria, he undertook to translate this work into Greek and completed his task sometime before 100 B.C. It was his translation, rather than the Hebrew original, which gained wide circulation and was eventually received into the Christian canon of Scripture.

#1: To demonstrate his command of Greek rhetoric the translator begins his Prologue with a long-winded and elaborate sentence, which RSV has translated literally. But for the translated text which follows the Prologue he uses a much simpler and more Biblical style. The Gospel of Luke begins in a similar way; we are reminded as well of the flowery prologue in 2 Mac 2:19-32. "The law and the prophets and the other books ..." (the writer repeats the phrase three times) indicates the threefold division of the Hebrew scriptures, which was already familiar to Ben Sira himself; cf.39:1. "The law" meant the five books ascribed to

Moses: Genesis, Exodus, Leviticus, Numbers, Deuteronomy. "The prophets" comprised both "the former prophets," now usually called "the historical books": Joshua, Judges, Samuel and Kings; and "the later prophets," prophetical books in the stricter sense: Isaiah, Jeremiah, Ezekiel, and the book of the Twelve, i.e. the "minor prophets." Finally, "the other books" are what later Jews called "the Writings"; this third collection was headed by Psalms, Proverbs and Job, but in Ben Sira's time it was still "open," i.e. new titles might be added to it. The Jewish canon of Scripture was not finally "closed" till about 100 A.D. But by the late 2nd century B.C. all the books considered holy and authoritative had been translated into Greek, since the Egyptian Jews could no longer understand Hebrew. These translations are known collectively as the Septuagint; the translator had obviously familiarized himself with them, as models for his own work. He also lays stress on Ben Sira's long preparation for his work, "devoting himself ... acquiring proficiency ...," and the motives of charity and zeal which inspired him to the composition of such a lengthy and all-embracing work of "instruction and wisdom."

#3, "opportunity for no little instruction" is a phrase of uncertain meaning. A better interpretation would be "no small difference in religious formation," meaning that the Egyptian Jews did not have as high a standard of religious practice as those in Judea. Therefore "it seemed highly necessary, etc.".

#2 brings the Prologue to an end with a humble request for indulgence towards any defects or errors in the translation. It is true that the translator has occasionally missed the meaning of the Hebrew; but on the whole his work was done with sufficient competence and great conscientiousness. By his third reference to "law ... prophecies, and the rest ... " we see that he was also familiar with the text of the Septuagint referred to above.

This appealing and candid preface puts us in touch, across so many centuries, with two men who set an inspiring example of unselfish service of the word of God. Each in his generation, they devoted years of their lives, with no thought of personal gain, to a labor which they judged to be to the greater glory of God and for the good of their neighbors. If we read no further than this Prologue, we should already have received an insight into the loving "fear of the Lord" which is the beginning of wisdom.

# I

## PRAISE OF WISDOM
1:1-30

### Origin from God
1:1-10

1All wisdom comes from the Lord
and is with him for ever.
2The sand of the sea, the drops of rain,
and the days of eternity — who
can count them?
3The height of heaven, the breadth
of the earth,
the abyss, and wisdom — who
can search them out?
4Wisdom was created before all things,
and prudent understanding from eternity.
6The root of wisdom — to whom has
it been revealed?
Her clever devices — who knows them?
8There is One who is wise, greatly
to be feared,
sitting upon his throne.
9The Lord himself created wisdom;
he saw her and apportioned her,
he poured her out upon all his works.

> [10]She dwells with all flesh according
>    to his gift,
>    and he supplied her to those
>    who love him.

These eight verses sum up Ben Sira's doctrine on Wisdom as a religious reality. The points outlined here will be developed more fully further on in the book. There is first the divine origin of Wisdom herself: she comes from the Lord, she is his creation and possession, she ever remains with him. Obviously this is divine Wisdom, an attribute of God himself, quite unattainable by human research or reflection. It is not, that is, any of the lower human levels of wisdom, such as skill, dexterity, diplomacy, insight into character, shrewdness and the like. Ben Sira stresses the inaccessibility of divine Wisdom by a series of comparisons: in vv. 2 and 3 are listed some natural phenomena of the physical universe. Already these are beyond human comprehension or measurement. How much more the Wisdom which belongs to the Lord alone and is comprehended only by him (vv. 8-9); St. Paul utters a similar cry of admiration in Rom 11:33.

This doctrine on divine Wisdom was already outlined at least in Prov 8:22-31 and Job 28:1-27, and presumably was known to Ben Sira's first readers. But he goes a step further: his conclusion (v. 10) is unexpectedly positive and encouraging. No merely human efforts can secure this great treasure; but what if the Lord freely bestows it on humankind? In fact, that is just what he has done and continues to do.

This was already laid down in Proverbs, where Wisdom, personified as a woman, pressingly invites all the children of men to profit by her teachings and conform their lives to her instructions (Prov 1:20ff, 8:1ff). That personification is continued by Ben Sira throughout this book. In this chapter, notice the feminine pronouns in vv. 6, 9f, 14-17. In remarkable contrast to the exclusivism of most pagan philosophies of the time, the Wisdom of Israel's God is insistently urged upon his people.

In v. 10 "all flesh" is to be understood as the human race in general, which accordingly has or can have a share in this gift; but the phrase "those who love him" specifies the covenant people of Israel, who by privilege of their election have a still greater share. This prepares for Ben Sira's special doctrine (chap. 24) that the making of that covenant was in fact the revelation of divine Wisdom. The Law of Moses *is* Wisdom. The "pouring out" of this Wisdom echoes the "pouring out" of the Spirit in Joel 3:1f; cf. also Acts 2:17, 33.

Wisdom and Fear of the Lord
1:11-20

$^{11}$The fear of the Lord is glory and exultation,
 and gladness and a crown of rejoicing.
$^{12}$The fear of the Lord delights the heart,
 and gives gladness and joy and long life.
$^{13}$With him who fears the Lord it will go well at the end;
 on the day of his death he will be blessed.
$^{14}$To fear the Lord is the beginning of wisdom;
 she is created with the faithful in the womb.
$^{15}$She made among men an eternal foundation,
 and among their descendants she will be trusted.
$^{16}$To fear the Lord is wisdom's full measure;
 she satisfies men with her fruits;
$^{17}$she fills their whole house with desirable goods,
 and their storehouses with her produce.
$^{18}$The fear of the Lord is the crown of wisdom,
 making peace and perfect health to flourish.
$^{19}$He saw her and apportioned her;
 he rained down knowledge and
 discerning comprehension,
 and he exalted the glory of those who held her fast.
$^{20}$To fear the Lord is the root of wisdom,
 and her branches are long life.

Verses 11-13 are a transition passage. We have just heard that the Lord lavishes wisdom upon his friends; but these friends are free agents, responsible creatures, and they must be properly prepared to receive his gift. The human disposition which corresponds to the divine bounty is summed up in the classical phrase, "the fear of the Lord." By this of course is not meant a servile or cringing fear, much less terror; it is profound reverence before his greatness, justice and goodness, combined with devotion and gratitude.

In vv. 14-20 Ben Sira is insisting, with a profusion of poetic images, on the connection between that "fear" and the reception and enjoyment of divine Wisdom. The former is Wisdom's beginning, fullness, crown and root. The first of these was a familiar slogan among Israel's sages: cf. Job 28:28, Prov 1:7, 9:10, Ps 111:10. The other three seem to be Ben Sira's "variations on the theme"; see below 21:11.

## How One Acquires Wisdom
## 1:22-30

22Unrighteous anger cannot be justified,
for a man's anger tips the scale to his ruin.
23A patient man will endure until the right moment,
and then joy will burst forth for him.
24He will hide his words until the right moment,
and the lips of many will tell of his good sense.
25In the treasuries of wisdom are wise sayings,
but godliness is an abomination to a sinner.
26If you desire wisdom, keep the commandments,
and the Lord will supply it for you.
27For the fear of the Lord is wisdom
and instruction,
and he delights in fidelity and meekness.
28Do not disobey the fear of the Lord;
do not approach him with a divided mind.
29Be not a hypocrite in men's sight,
and keep watch over your lips.
30Do not exalt yourself lest you fall,
and thus bring dishonor upon yourself.
The Lord will reveal your secrets
and cast you down in the midst of the congregation,
because you did not come in the fear of the Lord,
and your heart was full of deceit.

Verses 22-24 are another transition. The "patient man" of v. 23 corresponds to the God-fearer of v. 13, and his "good sense" (24) equals the fear of the Lord.

Verses 25-27, 28-30, are two strophes in the hortatory style typical of wisdom writing. The hearer or reader is addressed in the masculine singular, as an adolescent or young man who is sitting at the feet of the sage, eager to imbibe the wisdom which will give him the key to happy and successful living. He receives a mixture of encouragement and warning. Verse 25 is the first example of antithetic parallelism; the second colon begins with "but." Verses 26-27 develop the positive statement in v. 25a, while vv. 28-30 develop the negative in v. 25b.

Verse 26 sums up the doctrine of the chapter; a close parallel, perhaps a quotation, is found in Mt 19:17, "If you wish to enter into life, keep the commandments." 28-20 warn against insincerity, hypocrisy and pride — in short, religious formalism as depicted in the Gospels. "Keeping the commandments" in the sight of others *can* co-exist with hidden vices, as we all know. Hence the need for "fidelity and meekness" (v. 27). Again, there is an echo at least of v. 30ab in Mt 23:12: "Whoever exalts himself shall be humbled."

## RELATIONSHIP TO GOD
2:1-18

A perennial problem for the wisdom writers was the familiar one of retribution in this life. If Israel's God was all-powerful, all-knowing, loving and just, why should there be so much injustice, so much innocent suffering, on this earth, in human life, and especially among his covenant people? Why should devout God-fearing Jews so often be oppressed and persecuted, while their tormentors either were servants of false gods or worshiped no gods at all? If Israel had a covenant with the Lord, then according to the ideas of the time that covenant-God, her suzerain, was bound to care for his vassals to the utmost of his ability, to protect and shelter them, provided always they were faithful to their obligations under the covenant. In Israel's case that meant fidelity to the law of Moses, specifically the Ten

Commandments. In pre-Exilic times the great prophets had accounted for military defeats, for drought or famine or pestilence, by denouncing the general infidelity of the population to the will of the Lord — whether in terms of the non-observance of the Commandments (Amos, Hosea) or of rejection of the will of God made known to them through the prophets themselves (Isaiah, Jeremiah).

In part, this tradition of denouncing collective guilt as cause of collective suffering revived after the Exile (in Joel and Malachi). But changed circumstances made it seem less convincing. The little community of Judeans in and around the rebuilt Jerusalem, from the time of Ezra on, was isolated from the pagans and strictly observant of the Mosaic law. On the other hand, it was not so much collective suffering as affliction of individuals in the midst of security and plenty that caused the problem to remain acute.

Some maintained, in the teeth of contrary evidence, that the pious never did suffer; cf. Ps 37:25:

> I have been young, and now am old;
> yet I have not seen the righteous forsaken
> or his children begging bread.

The danger here was that if a man was clearly seen to be "forsaken," one might conclude that he had never been really righteous at all. That was the outrageous and calumnious judgment passed upon Job by his friends.

A more humane solution might be the theory of "medicinal suffering," which is stressed in the book of Job by Elihu (Job 32-37). He urges that suffering may be sent by God to remind people of their fallibility and weakness, and to guard them against presumption and neglecting to pray to God.

A more rewarding interpretation was that arrived at by the author of Ps 73, who candidly records his scandal at the prosperity of the godless, while he, faithful to his religious duties, found himself poor and helpless. By the grace of God he achieved the insight that his relationship to his Lord was itself the greatest of goods, which no one could take from him but which the godless did not enjoy.

Thou dost guide me with thy counsel,
and afterward thou wilt receive me to glory.
Whom have I in heaven but thee?
And there is nothing upon earth
that I desire besides thee (Ps 73:24-25).

This was the problem which Ben Sira courageously faced, immediately after his prologue in chap. 1. He sets an admirable example of honesty and candor in facing up to it, not trying to sweep it under the rug but offering the best solution that he can.

2 My Son, if you come forward
to serve the Lord,
prepare yourself for temptation.
2Set your heart right and be steadfast,
and do not be hasty in time of calamity.
3Cleave to him and do not depart,
that you may be honored at the end of your life.
4Accept whatever is brought upon you,
and in changes that humble you be patient.
5For gold is tested in the fire,
and acceptable men in the furnace of humiliation.
6Trust in him, and he will help you;
make your ways straight and hope in him.
7You who fear the Lord, wait for his mercy;
and turn not aside, lest you fall.
8You who fear the Lord, trust in him,
and your reward will not fail;
9you who fear the Lord, hope for good things,
for everlasting joy and mercy.
10Consider the ancient generations and see:
who ever trusted in the Lord and was put to shame?
Or who ever persevered in the fear of the Lord
and was forsaken?
Or who ever called upon him and was overlooked?
11For the Lord is compassionate and merciful;
he forgives sins and saves in time of affliction.

The discourse begins with the traditional pedagogic address to one hearer, "my son," frequently used in Prov 1-7. The exhortation of master to disciple was introduced this way. But from v. 7 on the instruction turns into a sort of chant addressed to a plurality, and ends in the 1st person plural, "us," in v. 18. Wisdom is not mentioned in this chapter at all; fear of the Lord takes its place, and instead of acquiring wisdom we hear of coming to serve the Lord. Ben Sira shifts from the idea of profit or self-interest, which might arise from chap. 1, to the concept of moral obligation. Skillfully he interweaves the ideas of heaven-sent affliction, of covenant loyalty, of love and faithfulness to the divine call. First he admits, or rather straightforwardly affirms, that faithfulness to the known will of God is not a guarantee of prosperity and happiness; on the contrary it will regularly involve trials and adversity. These are to be interpreted as tests of the God-fearer's sincerity and devotion; they are to be borne with patience, and in the conviction that they will be temporary. They will give place to reward, to "everlasting joy and mercy." Two of the NT epistles start with similar warnings: Jas 1:2f, 1 Pet 1:6f.; the latter also uses the image of testing gold by melting it down in a furnace. Verse 6 uses another favorite wisdom expression, "making ways straight"; the image of a "right path" along which one must at every step "direct" one's way was a familiar symbol of human life considered as a series of moral choices (*cf.* Ps 1:6).

In vv. 7-9 the theme of "fearing the Lord" is picked up from chap. 1. Waiting, trust and hope are three expressions of the right attitude to be adopted by the faithful who "come forward to serve the Lord." Verses 10-11 call on the witness of history to prove Ben Sira's thesis and dispel all doubts. We may see here with what "eyes of faith" Ben Sira read the historical books narrating the experiences of the patriarchs, the ancestors and the people of God in general. He will provide a grandiose elaboration of that history in chaps. 44-49. Here he appeals to its record of prayer uttered and answered. The answer to the three questions in v. 10 would of course according to Ben Sira have been "No one." He does not comment on objections that might be made, notably the premature death of the good king Josiah — which the Chronicler had felt the need to explain as caused by disobedience to the word of God: 2 Chr 35:21f.

Verse 11 gives in brief form what may be called a "definition" of the Lord, a formula much loved and often repeated in the sacred writings. It occurs first in Exod 34:6, "The Lord, the Lord, a God merciful and gracious, slow to anger and abounding in steadfast love and faithfulness . . . "and is echoed in about 15 other passages.

> [12]Woe to timid hearts and to slack hands,
>     and to the sinner who walks along two ways!
> [13]Woe to the faint heart, for it has no trust!
>     Therefore it will not be sheltered.
> [14]Woe to you who have lost your endurance!
>     What will you do when the Lord punishes you?
> [15]Those who fear the Lord will not disobey his words,
>     and those who love him will keep his ways.
> [16]Those who fear the Lord will seek his approval,
>     and those who love him will be filled with the law.
> [17]Those who fear the Lord will prepare their hearts,
>     and will humble themselves before him.
> [18]Let us fall into the hands of the Lord,
>     but not into the hands of men;
>     for as his majesty is, so also is his mercy.

Verses 12-14 adopt a figure which is the opposite of the Beatitude: the Woe. This was popular with some of the prophets; cf. Amos 5:7, 18; 6:1; Isa 5:8ff. Here it is a negative contrast to the encouragement of vv. 7-9; these apostates do not hope nor trust, so must expect punishment. Ben Sira no doubt has in mind the numerous Jews, especially of the wealthy and ruling classes, who had so far adopted hellenistic culture and manners as to abandon in part or in whole observance of the Mosaic law. A generation later their behavior and attitudes are clearly pictured in 1 Mac 1:11ff., 2 Mac 4:7ff.

Verses 15-17 return to the praise of the God-fearers, this time in the 3rd person. Note that Ben Sira twice puts in parallelism "Those who fear the Lord"with "those who love him." Clearly, to him the two expressions mean the same. In v. 16 is his first mention of the Law, which later on he will identify with Wisdom herself. But we may remark right away that Ben Sira does not conceive this Wisdom-Law as a code of external observances to be fenced around with an elaborate system of casuistry. To be "filled with the law"(v. 16) is to have a constant and effective desire to find the will of God and to act upon it.

In conclusion, the two couplets of v. 18 are a beautiful expression of the virtue of trust; cf. v. 6. "To fall into the hands of"is a frequent Hebrew expression usually meaning a calamity leading to destruction or death; e.g. Ps 31:8, 78:61. Ben Sira neatly transforms it into an image of rescue and salvation. The "hands" of the Lord are instruments of his mercy, i.e. of his covenant love.

## RESPECT FOR PARENTS
3:1-16

3 Listen to me your father, O children;
   and act accordingly, that you
   may be kept in safety.
²For the Lord honored the father above the children,
   and he confirmed the right of the mother over her sons.
³Whoever honors his father atones for sins,
⁴   and whoever glorifies his mother
   is like one who lays up treasure.
⁵Whoever honors his father will be gladdened by his own children,
   and when he prays he will be heard.
⁶Whoever glorifies his father will have long life,
   and whoever obeys the Lord will refresh his mother;
⁷   he will serve his parents as his masters.
⁸Honor your father by word and deed,
   that a blessing from him may come upon you.
⁹For a father's blessing strengthens
   the houses of the children,
      but a mother's curse uproots their foundations.

10Do not glorify yourself by
   dishonoring your father,
   for your father's dishonor is no glory to you.
11For a man's glory comes from
   honoring his father,
   and it is a disgrace for children
   not to respect their mother.
12O son, help your father in his old age,
   and do not grieve him as long as he lives;
13even if he is lacking in understanding,
   show forbearance;
   in all your strength do not despise him.
14For kindness to a father will not be forgotten,
   and against your sins it will be credited to you;
15in the day of your affliction it will
   be remembered in your favor;
   as frost in fair weather, your sins
   will melt away.
16Whoever forsakes his father is like a blasphemer,
   and whoever angers his mother is cursed by the Lord.

Having dealt with the pursuit of wisdom in general (chap. 1) and the need of loyalty to the ancestral religion (chap. 2), Ben Sira now turns to the first of his "practical" subjects, which turns out to be the duty of loving and honoring one's parents. In these opening chapters of his book it is clear that he has chiefly in mind young people, adolescents, not yet married, still living in the parents' home; but his instruction is valid also for adults with aged parents, cf. v. 12. The subject had already been treated in Proverbs, but only in isolated verses and mainly negative terms. Ben Sira is apparently the first to have composed a commentary on the commandment, "Honor your father and your mother." He will return briefly to the topic in 7:27f. but chap. 3 is his only extended treatment of it. Note the repeated idea (vv. 3, 14f) that honoring parents serves to atone for sins.

## ON HUMILITY
3:17-29

> [17]My son, perform your tasks in meekness:
>    then you will be loved by those whom God accepts.
> [18]The greater you are, the more you
>    must humble yourself;
>    so you will find favor in the sight of the Lord.
> [20]For great is the might of the Lord;
>    he is glorified by the humble.
> [21]Seek not what is too difficult for you,
>    nor investigate what is beyond your power.
> [22]Reflect upon what has been assigned to you,
>    for you do not need what is hidden.
> [23]Do not meddle in what is beyond your tasks,
>    for matters too great for human
>    understanding have been shown you.
> [24]For their hasty judgment has led many astray,
>    and wrong opinion has caused their thoughts to slip.
> [26]A stubborn mind will be afflicted at the end,
>    and whoever loves danger will perish by it.
> [27]A stubborn mind will be burdened by troubles,
>    and the sinner will heap sin upon sin.
> [28]The affliction of the proud has no healing,
>    for a plant of wickedness has taken root in him.
> [29]The mind of the intelligent man
>    will ponder a parable,
>    and an attentive ear is the wise man's desire.

This warning against pride has an evangelical sound; it is like an advance commentary on the third of the Matthean beatitudes, "Blessed are the meek, for they shall inherit the earth." The motivation proposed is interesting: v. 17b, love from one's neighbor; v. 18b, favor with God. In vv. 21-23 the warning becomes more specific, yet the reference is obscure for us. Possibly it concerns various forms of Greek philosophy and the teaching of the sophists, which might have an attraction for young Greek-speaking Jews but would probably be looked on by Ben Sira as pagan doctrine incompatible with Judaism. In the early church these lines were quoted against gnostic heretics who claimed salvation by secret sources of knowledge, known only by the initiated.

## ON ALMSGIVING
## 3:30-4:10

$^{30}$Water extinguishes a blazing fire:
  so almsgiving atones for sin.
$^{31}$Whoever requites favors gives thought to the future;
  at the moment of his falling he will find support.

**4** My son, deprive not the poor of his living,
  and do not keep needy eyes waiting.
$^{2}$Do not grieve the one who is hungry,
  nor anger a man in want.
$^{3}$Do not add to the troubles of an angry mind,
  nor delay your gift to a beggar.
$^{4}$Do not reject an afflicted suppliant,
  nor turn your face away from the poor.
$^{5}$Do not avert your eye from the needy,
  nor give a man occasion to curse you;
$^{6}$for if in bitterness of soul he calls
  down a curse upon you,
  his Creator will hear his prayer.
$^{7}$Make yourself beloved in the congregation;
  bow your head low to a great man.
$^{8}$Incline your ear to the poor,
  and answer him peaceably and gently.
$^{9}$Deliver him who is wronged from
  the hand of the wrongdoer;
  and do not be fainthearted in judging a case.
$^{10}$Be like a father to orphans,
  and instead of a husband to their mother;
you will then be like a son of the Most High,
  and he will love you more than does your mother.

Ben Sira begins with another of his striking images: as water puts out fire, almsgiving atones for sins. We see here that the sage takes for granted his pupils will be sons of wealthy families, or at least not poverty-stricken and not likely to be in want. All the more he aims at inculcating social responsibility and the right use of wealth. In the culture of that time there was nothing remotely comparable to our "social services," operated by government agencies with taxpayers' money. Any provision there might be, of food, shelter, clothing or other necessities for the indigent and the destitute, was entirely a matter of private initiative and generosity. This is a theme that Ben Sira returns to repeatedly, and his concern for it is one of the most attractive aspects of his character. He shows no trace of the moral censure which was sometimes inferred from the crude doctrine that riches were a sign of God's blessing but poverty always punishment for sin. On the contrary, the poor are God's special friends (v. 6) and he will take their side. In 8-10ab courtesy and love are inculcated in dealing with the poor, with orphans, with widows. In the last phrase of the section, v. 10d, the Greek translator (followed by RSV) has improved on his original, which had only "will graciously save you from destruction." Perhaps he had in mind the famous passage Isa 49:15, "Can a woman forget her sucking child ...? Even these may forget, yet I will not forget you," and felt he could construct a better parallelism with more emotional appeal.

# II

## THE REWARDS OF WISDOM
## 4:11-19

[11]Wisdom exalts her sons
and gives help to those who seek her.
[12]Whoever loves her loves life,
and those who seek her early
will be filled with joy.
[13]Whoever holds her fast will obtain glory,
and the Lord will bless the place she enters.
[14]Those who serve her will minister to the Holy One;
the Lord loves those who love her.
[15]He who obeys her will judge the nations,
and whoever gives heed to her will dwell secure.
[16]If he has faith in her he will obtain her;
and his descendants will remain in possession of her.
[17]For at first she will walk with him on tortuous paths,
she will bring fear and cowardice upon him,
and will torment him by her discipline
until she trusts him,
and she will test him with her ordinances.
[18]Then she will come straight back to
him and gladden him,
and will reveal her secrets to him.
[19]If he goes astray she will forsake him,
and hand him over to his ruin.

In this, the second presentation of Lady Wisdom, the personification is more realistic than in chap. 1, and there is more stress on the aspect of trial, e.g. v. 17. We notice the "son of the Most High" (v. 10) is now a son of Wisdom (v. 11); there is no separation between the two. In the preceding section on almsgiving Ben Sira's instructions were practical and precise; here, they are general and wide-reaching. Wisdom's children are to seek her (twice), love her (twice), hold her fast, serve her, obey her, give heed to her, have faith in her. In turn, she will, after the testing, assure them of exaltation, help, joy, glory, the Lord's love, security, gladness.

## TRUE AND FALSE SHAME
4:20-28

Ben Sira, like all good teachers, is concerned to form as well as to inform the minds of his students. Wisdom for him is not merely the retention as in a well-stored computer of items of information, nor registration of and acquiescence in judgments, however solidly based, enunciated by the teacher. It is a skill by which students eventually are enabled to form their own judgments and make their own choices and decisions, just as competently as their mentor. One of Ben Sira's favorite techniques for stimulating mental activity in his neophytes is "illustrations by contrast." He likes to take one word or idea, and invite his listeners to distinguish between welcome and unwelcome aspects of the same. It is, in a way, an anticipation of the refined techniques of the mediaeval Schoolmen, with their distinctions and subdistinctions.

> 20Observe the right time, and beware of evil;
>     and do not bring shame on yourself.
> 21For there is a shame which brings sin,
>     and there is a shame which is glory and favor.
> 22Do not show partiality, to your own harm,
>     or deference, to your downfall.
> 23Do not refrain from speaking at the crucial time,
>     and do not hide your wisdom.

24For wisdom is known through speech,
  and education through the words of the tongue.
25Never speak against the truth,
  but be mindful of your ignorance.
26Do not be ashamed to confess your sins,
  and do not try to stop the current of a river.
27Do not subject yourself to a foolish fellow,
  nor show partiality to a ruler.
28Strive even to death for the truth
  and the Lord God will fight for you.

Verse 20 is a brief introduction; "of evil" is the same expression as at the end of the Lord's prayer, "deliver us *from evil*," Mt 6:13. Then Ben Sira sets out to clarify the ambiguity of "shame"; is this something good or bad? "Bad" or guilty shame is illustrated in vv. 22, 23, 26a, 27a; a young person might through diffidence or natural modesty hesitate to speak out when speech was called for. Honorable shame is illustrated in vv. 25, 26b, 27b, 28. It involves a proper self-respect, with readiness to admit one's mistakes. The concluding v. 28 is a surprisingly emphatic admonition; obviously Ben Sira here thinks of truth as a religious value, which is worth dying for. And indeed among his hearers there may well have been some — or many —who some twenty years later joined in the holy war of Judas Maccabeus and put their lives on the line "for truth."

## ON PRESUMPTION
4:29-5:8

29Do not be reckless in your speech,
  or sluggish and remiss in your deeds.
30Do not be like a lion in your home,
  nor be a faultfinder with your servants.
31Let not your hand be extended to receive,
  but withdrawn when it is time to repay.'

**5**  Do not set your heart on your wealth,
  nor say, "I have enough."

²Do not follow your inclination and strength,
  walking according to the desires of your heart.
³Do not say, "Who will have power over me?"
  for the Lord will surely punish you.
⁴Do not say, "I sinned, and what happened to me?"
  for the Lord is slow to anger.
⁵Do not be so confident of atonement
  that you add sin to sin.
⁶Do not say, "His mercy is great,
  he will forgive the multitude of my sins,"
for both mercy and wrath are with him
  and his anger rests on sinners.
⁷Do not delay to turn to the Lord,
  nor postpone it from day to day;
for suddenly the wrath of the Lord will go forth,
  and at the time of punishment you will perish.
⁸Do not depend on dishonest wealth,
  for it will not benefit you in the day of calamity.

This section, like the one following, is made up almost entirely of negative precepts, warning against over-confidence especially in religious matters. In v. 29 probably a contrast is intended: "Do not be reckless ... *but* sluggish ..." The very pointed v. 31 is quoted in the *Didache,* an early Christian liturgical composition from about 100 A.D. Ben Sira proceeds to argue against reliance on material possessions and wealth, as protecting the owner against even religious sanctions; and further, against out-and-out scepticism as to God's will or even power to punish sinners. This obviously was a live question — another form of the "problem of retribution" — and Ben Sira's young hearers would no doubt have been exposed to some very cynical arguments on the question. He tackles the problem in lively and dramatic fashion, quoting four sayings (vv. 1, 3, 4, 6) which presumably were in wide circulation. The fourth one is tantamount to a refusal to repent, as not being necessary: "Of course God will forgive my sins; that's his job."

It is interesting to compare this sapiential style, of quiet yet serious and impressive admonition, with the fiery oratory and eloquent denunciations of the great prophets. The difference of course is in the setting: for the sage, a small group of young auditors in the "house of instruction" (51:23); for the prophet, a tumultuous and often resentful or mocking crowd in the city square or the temple court. Each style, we may conclude, was well adapted and effective in its setting.

## CONSISTENT SPEECH
5:9-6:1

$^9$Do not winnow with every wind,
   nor follow every path:
   the double-tongued sinner does that.
$^{10}$Be steadfast in your understanding,
   and let your speech be consistent.
$^{11}$Be quick to hear,
   and be deliberate in answering.
$^{12}$If you have understanding, answer your neighbor;
   but if not, put your hand on your mouth.
$^{13}$Glory and dishonor come from speaking,
   and a man's tongue is his downfall.
$^{14}$Do not be called a slanderer,
   and do not lie in ambush with your tongue;
for shame comes to the thief,
   and severe condemnation to the double-tongued.
$^{15}$In great or small matters do not act amiss,
   and do not become an enemy instead of a friend;
6   for a bad name incurs shame and reproach:
   so fares the double-tongued sinner.

This is the first section in the book treating of the right and moral use of the faculty of speech. It will not be the last. Like the authors of Proverbs, Ben Sira is keenly aware of the enormous influence for good or evil in human society of the right and wrong use of the tongue. Cf. in the NT the Epistle of James (3:1-12), which of all the NT writings is closest in form and substance to the book of Ben Sira. The latter is never tired of urging tact and discretion, kindness and consideration, in all verbal contacts with our neighbors.

The first phrase in v. 9 is probably a familiar proverb which Ben Sira can turn to his purpose. The process of winnowing grain, after the thrashing, was performed on an elevation when a steady wind was blowing. The mixed mass of grain and chaff was tossed in the air with fans, the light chaff blew away with the wind, the heavier grain fell back on the ground. But for this operation changing or veering winds would be worse than useless. Verse 11 is quoted in Jas 1:19. Verse 13 is another example of the need of discernment; speech, like so many other things, can be good or bad. The phrase is echoed in Jas 3:10, "From the same mouth come blessing and cursing. My brethren, this ought not to be so."

## SELF-CONTROL
6:2-4

> 2Do not exalt yourself through your soul's counsel,
>   lest your soul be torn in pieces like a bull.
> 3You will devour your leaves and destroy your fruit,
>   and will be left like a withered tree.
> 4An evil soul will destroy him who has it,
>   and make him the laughingstock of his enemies.

This is a transition passage, passing from right use of the tongue in general to the importance of kindly speech to maintain friendship. In between is this call to self-control against any violent passion; the species does not matter —lust, greed, anger or the like. With the picturesque comparison of a tree being devastated by fire Ben Sira makes his point about the danger of "losing control."

## TRUE FRIENDSHIP
6:5-17

> 5A pleasant voice multiplies friends,
>   and a gracious tongue multiplies courtesies.
> 6Let those that are at peace with you be many,
>   but let your advisers be one in a thousand.
> 7When you gain a friend, gain him through testing,
>   and do not trust him hastily.

[8]For there is a friend who is such
at his own convenience,
but will not stand by you in
your day of trouble.
[9]And there is a friend who changes into an enemy,
and will disclose a quarrel to your disgrace.
[10]And there is a friend who is a table companion,
but will not stand by you in your day of trouble.
[11]In your prosperity he will make himself your equal,
and be bold with your servants;
[12]but if you are brought low he will turn against you,
and will hide himself from your presence.
[13]Keep yourself far from your enemies,
and be on guard toward your friends.
[14]A faithful friend is a sturdy shelter:
he that has found one has found a treasure.
[15]There is nothing so precious as a faithful friend,
and no scales can measure his excellence.
[16]A faithful friend is an elixir of life;
and those who fear the Lord will find him.
[17]Whoever fears the Lord directs his friendship aright,
for as he is, so is his neighbor also.

This is another of Ben Sira's favorite topics, to which he will return in 9:10-16, 11:29-12:18, 22:19-26, 37:1-6. Not only is this topic very important in the training of youth, but Ben Sira's lines in vv. 6-8 were quoted in the Talmud and in a later Jewish sage, Saadia Gaon. Again there is need for discernment; "a faithful friend is ... a treasure," but few evidently are faithful. After the introduction (v. 5) with mention of the importance of courteous speech Ben Sira warns against three kinds of false friends, vv. 8-12. He winds up the section with warm praise of the true friend, vv. 14-17, and as usual ends with reference (vv. 16-17) to the religious values which are always supposed behind his down-to-earth admonitions.

# III

## RECOMMENDATION OF WISDOM
6:18-37

[18]My son, from your youth up choose instruction,
  and until you are old you will keep finding wisdom.
[19]Come to her like one who plows and sows,
  and wait for her good harvest.
For in her service you will toil a little while,
  and soon you will eat of her produce.
[20]She seems very harsh to the uninstructed;
  a weakling will not remain with her.
[21]She will weigh him down like a heavy testing stone,
  and he will not be slow to cast her off.
[22]For wisdom is like her name,
  and is not manifest to many.

[23]Listen, my son, and accept my judgment;
  do not reject my counsel.
[24]Put your feet into her fetters,
  and your neck into her collar.
[25]Put your shoulder under her and carry her,
  and do not fret under her bonds.
[26]Come to her with all your soul,
  and keep her ways with all your might.
[27]Search out and seek, and she will become known to you;
  and when you get hold of her, do not let her go.

28For at last you will find the rest she gives,
  and she will be changed into joy for you.
29Then her fetters will become for
  you a strong protection,
  and her collar a glorious robe.
30Her yoke is a golden ornament,
  and her bonds are a cord of blue.
31You will wear her like a glorious robe,
  and put her on like a crown of gladness.

32If you are willing, my son, you will be taught,
  and if you apply yourself you will become clever.
33If you love to listen you will gain knowledge,
  and if you incline your ear you will become wise.
34Stand in the assembly of the elders.
  Who is wise? Cleave to him.
35Be ready to listen to every narrative,
  and do not let wise proverbs escape you.
36If you see an intelligent man, visit him early;
  let your foot wear out his doorstep.
37Reflect on the statutes of the Lord,
  and meditate at all times on his commandments.
It is he who will give insight to your mind,
  and your desire for wisdom will be granted.

For the third time Ben Sira turns to the analysis of wisdom, as the greatest good and blessing in human life. Here he comes forward to speak in his own person, in intimate man-to-man counseling of a single pupil. The address "my son" marks off three subdivisions of the address (vv. 18, 23, 32). Under a variety of images, the first two stress the laborious, even painful, beginnings of this study (vv. 20f., 24f.); but it will issue in "rest ... joy ... a glorious robe ... a crown of gladness." The passage is echoed in Mt 11:28-30, where Jesus speaking as divine Wisdom incarnate utters a similar call and promise. In the third subdivision, vv. 32-37, without any metaphoric language (but with one hyperbole, v. 36b!), Ben Sira explains in detail how the neophyte is to arrive at wisdom. As always, he combines commonsensical human means (vv. 33-36) with the infusion of divine grace (v. 37). Both in his view are necessary. We see here how different "schools" of wisdom existed among the rabbis of the time. In 51:23 the author will recommend his own "house of instruction," but here Ben Sira is willing to leave to his student the choice of any "intelligent man."

## NEGATIVE PRECEPTS
7:1-17

**7**  Do no evil, and evil will never befall you.
2Stay away from wrong, and it will turn away from you.
3My son, do not sow the furrows of injustice,
   and you will not reap a sevenfold crop.
4Do not seek from the Lord the highest office,
   nor the seat of honor from the king.
5Do not assert your righteousness before the Lord,
   nor display your wisdom before the king.
6Do not seek to become a judge,
   lest you be unable to remove iniquity,
lest you be partial to a powerful man,
   and thus put a blot on your integrity.
7Do not offend against the public,
   and do not disgrace yourself among the people.
8Do not commit a sin twice;
   even for one you will not go unpunished.
9Do not say, "He will consider the multitude of my gifts,
   and when I make an offering to the Most High God
   he will accept it."
10Do not be fainthearted in your prayer,
   nor neglect to give alms.
11Do not ridicule a man who is bitter in soul,
   for there is One who abases and exalts.
12Do not devise a lie against your brother,
   nor do the like to a friend.
13Refuse to utter any lie,
   for the habit of lying serves no good.
14Do not prattle in the assembly of the elders,
   nor repeat yourself in your prayer.

[15]Do not hate toilsome labor,
　　or farm work, which were
　　created by the Most High.
[16]Do not count yourself among the crowd of sinners;
　　remember that wrath does not delay.
[17]Humble yourself greatly,
　　for the punishment of the ungodly is fire and worms.

In 15 successive prohibitions Ben Sira lays down a code of moral behavior concerned especially with principles of social ethics. Verses 1-3 give general principles, already linked with a doctrine of retribution, and the remaining vv. give specific applications. Verse 4 adds a religious note to Prov 25:6, "Do not put yourself forward in the king's presence, or stand in the place of the great," and both are echoed in the Gospels, Lk 14:10 and parallel passages. Verse 6 shows Ben Sira's realism; like the Delphic oracle he recommends "Know yourself." A judge in that society would need great strength and integrity of character to withstand the moral or financial pressure which unscrupulous litigants might bring to bear on him. Verses 8-9 return momentarily to the presumption theme, as in 5:4-7. Verse 11 anticipates the call to compassion in 8:5-7. Verse 14, restraint and brevity in prayer had already been recommended by Ecclesiastes, 5:2, and the warning is repeated in Jesus' words, Mt 6:7f. Verse 15 is another example of Ben Sira's balanced judgment. Though he believed in a hierarchy of trades and professions, and put his own avocation of scribe and Scripture student in first place, he would not allow handicrafts and manual labor to be belittled or despised. See his discussion in 38:24-34. Verse 17, the passage ends with a somber reproach to all human pride and pretensions. Ben Sira, who had no concept of a judgment after death or possible happy immortality, wrote "for the expectation of man is worms." The grandson, who did believe in a judgment, changed this to read as the RSV has it.

## PERSONAL RELATIONSHIPS
7:18-36

[18]Do not exchange a friend for money,
    or a real brother for the gold of Ophir.
[19]Do not deprive yourself of a wise and good wife,
    for her charm is worth more than gold.
[20]Do not abuse a servant
    who performs his work faithfully,
    or a hired laborer who devotes himself to you.
[21]Let your soul love an intelligent servant;
    do not withhold from him his freedom.
[22]Do you have cattle? Look after them;
    if they are profitable to you, keep them.
[23]Do you have children? Discipline them,
    and make them obedient from their youth.
[24]Do you have daughters?
    Be concerned for their chastity,
    and do not show yourself too indulgent with them.
[25]Give a daughter in marriage;
    you will have finished a great task.
    But give her to a man of understanding.
[26]If you have a wife who pleases you, do not cast her out;
    but do not trust yourself to one whom you detest.
[27]With all your heart honor your father,
    and do not forget the birth pangs of your mother.
[28]Remember that through your parents you were born;
    and what can you give back to them
    that equals their gift to you?
[29]With all your soul fear the Lord,
    and honor his priests.
[30]With all your might love your Maker,
    and do not forsake his ministers.
[31]Fear the Lord and honor the priest,
    and give him his portion, as is commanded you:
the first fruits, the guilt offering,
    the gift of the shoulders,
the sacrifice of sanctification,
    and the first fruits of the holy things.
[32]Stretch forth your hand to the poor,

so that your blessing may be complete.
33Give graciously to all the living,
and withhold not kindness from the dead.
34Do not fail those who weep,
but mourn with those who mourn.
35Do not shrink from visiting a sick man,
because for such deeds you will be loved.
36In all you do, remember the end of your life,
and then you will never sin.

Verses 18-28 survey relationships within the family, rather sketchily; they mention successively a friend, a brother, a wife, a slave, a hired man, and livestock; then, sons and daughters; then an untrustworthy wife; finally, parents. In v. 20a and v. 21a "servant" is really "slave," as shown by the reference to "freedom." The Mosaic law (Ex 21:2, Deut 15:12) prescribed the manumission of Hebrew slaves after six years; they were to be released with generous gifts. It is typical of Ben Sira's concern for oppressed members of society that he should mention this point, and apparently wish the law to be applied also to Gentile slaves. In v. 23 the Hebrew text reads, "Do you have sons? ... Choose wives for them while they are young." This is correct, and corresponds to v. 25.

Verses 29-31 concern religious duties. Three times Ben Sira puts in parallel "the Lord/your Maker" with "his priests/ministers," as though to stress that sincere worship of the former involves reverence and support for the latter. He himself was probably not a priest, but he had a great love for the Temple liturgy, and high admiration for those members of the clergy whom he judged to be conscientious and faithful. See his panegyric on the high priest Simon, chap. 50, and his respectful but pointed admonition to the Levite priests of his time, 45:26. Verse 31, "give him his portion" is a very practical directive, equivalent to "contribute to the support of your pastors." Temples in the ancient world did not usually have endowments, and if worshipers ceased coming, and contributing, to a particular shrine, its priesthood might perforce scatter to earn a living elsewhere, and all public worship of that particular deity would come to an end. Since the Jerusalem temple was (according to the letter of the law) the only place where sacrificial worship might be offered to the God of Israel, Ben Sira is concerned that it be adequately supported. Whether the temple tax, established in the time of Nehemiah (Neh 10:33; cf. Mt 17:24ff.), was being collected in Ben Sira's time we cannot be sure.

Verses 32-35 concern charity to all those in need: the poor, the deceased (presumably by due funeral rites and proper burial), mourners, the sick. Verse 34 is cited by Paul in Rom 12:15, and v. 35 is echoed in Mt 25:36. Verse 36a alludes to happiness at the moment of death, which Ben Sira considered to be of great importance; see 11:26-28.

## DEALINGS WITH OTHER MEN
8:1-19

**8** Do not contend with a powerful man,
   lest you fall into his hands.
2 Do not quarrel with a rich man,
   lest his resources outweigh yours;
for gold has ruined many,
   and has perverted the minds of kings.
3 Do not argue with a chatterer,
   nor heap wood on his fire.
4 Do not jest with an ill-bred person,
   lest your ancestors be disgraced.
5 Do not reproach a man who is turning away from sin;
   remember that we all deserve punishment.
6 Do not disdain a man when he is old,
   for some of us are growing old.
7 Do not rejoice over any one's death;
   remember that we all must die.
8 Do not slight the discourse of the sages,
   but busy yourself with their maxims;
because from them you will gain instruction
   and learn how to serve great men.
9 Do not disregard the discourse of the aged,
   for they themselves learned from their fathers;
because from them you will gain understanding

and learn how to give an answer in time of need.
$^{10}$Do not kindle the coals of a sinner,
    lest you be burned in his flaming fire.
$^{11}$Do not get up and leave an insolent fellow,
    lest he lie in ambush against your words.
$^{12}$Do not lend to a man who is stronger than you;
    but if you do lend anything, be as one who has lost it.
$^{13}$Do not give surety beyond your means,
    but if you give surety, be concerned as one who must
    pay.
$^{14}$Do not go to law against a judge,
    for the decision will favor him because of his standing.
$^{15}$Do not travel on the road with a foolhardy fellow,
    lest he be burdensome to you;
for he will act as he pleases,
    and through his folly you will perish with him.
$^{16}$Do not fight with a wrathful man,
    and do not cross the wilderness with him;
because blood is as nothing in his sight,
    and where no help is at hand,
    he will strike you down.
$^{17}$Do not consult with a fool,
    for he will not be able to keep a secret.
$^{18}$In the presence of a stranger
    do nothing that is to be kept secret,
    for you do not know what he will divulge.
$^{19}$Do not reveal your thoughts to every one,
    lest you drive away your good luck.

This chapter begins (vv. 1-4) and ends (vv. 10-19) with specific warnings against associating with various dishonest or dangerous characters; the list numbers twelve. In between are two briefer sections, vv. 5-7 and 8-9.

Verses 1-4 suppose that the young listener is not rich nor influential, nor able to assert himself against older men. The danger noted in 2b is probably that the rich man may be able to bribe a judge to decide against you. In v. 4b, the danger is of hearing a curse pronounced on your ancestors which you are powerless to avert or avenge.

Verses 5-7 show Ben Sira's humanism at its best. These gentle and compassionate reminders, this all-embracing human sympathy, easily compensate for some limitations elsewhere, due more to his training than to his own kind heart. Verse 7a intends specifically the death of one who has injured you. In 28:1-7 Ben Sira will develop a beautiful doctrine on forgiveness.

Verses 8-9 again invite the young man to profit from the instruction of the wise and aged. Verse 8d is (in the Hebrew) a quotation from Prov 22:29b. With v. 10 the warnings resume, dealing in practical terms with the dangers of lending money, going surety for others, bad traveling companions, etc.

(In v. 19a NAB has a strange mistake: "Open your heart to no man. . . " It should of course be "Open not your heart to every man . . . ")

## RELATIONS WITH WOMEN
9:1-9

**9**   Do not be jealous of the wife of your bosom,
    and do not teach her an evil lesson to your own hurt.
2 Do not give yourself to a woman
    so that she gains mastery over your strength.
3 Do not go to meet a loose woman,
    lest you fall into her snares.
4 Do not associate with a woman singer,
    lest you be caught in her intrigues.
5 Do not look intently at a virgin,
    lest you stumble and incur penalties for her.
6 Do not give yourself to harlots
    lest you lose your inheritance.
7 Do not look around in the streets of a city,
    nor wander about in its deserted sections.
8 Turn away your eyes from a shapely woman,
    and do not look intently at
      beauty belonging to another;
    many have been misled by a woman's beauty,
    and by it passion is kindled like a fire.

9Never dine with another man's wife,
   nor revel with her at wine;
lest your heart turn aside to her,
   and in blood you be plunged into destruction.

Ben Sira's warnings against loose sexual behavior were no doubt occasioned by the freer mores of the hellenistic culture in which his pupils lived their daily lives. He returns to the topic more at length in 25:13-26:18. Here, vv. 1-2 refer to marriage; v. 2 perhaps has reference to the bad example of Solomon, cf. 47:19 and 1 Kgs 11:4. The rest of the passage concerns other women, unmarried (vv. 3-7) or married to another (vv. 8-9). The "loose woman" in v. 3 is the figure described so picturesquely in Prov 2:16-19, 5:1-14, 6:24-7:27. Verse 5a, "look intently at a virgin" is the phrase used in Job 31:1.

## CHOICE OF FRIENDS
9:10-16

10Forsake not an old friend,
   for a new one does not compare with him.
A new friend is like new wine;
   when it has aged you will drink it with pleasure.
11Do not envy the honors of a sinner,
   for you do not know what his end will be.
12Do not delight in what pleases the ungodly;
   remember that they will not be held guiltless
      as long as they live.
13Keep far from a man who has the power to kill,
   and you will not be worried by the fear of death.
But if you approach him, make no misstep,
   lest he rob you of your life.
Know that you are walking in the midst of snares,
   and that you are going about on the city battlements.
14As much as you can, aim to know your neighbors,
   and consult with the wise.
15Let your conversation be with men of understanding,
   and let all your discussion be
      about the law of the Most High.

16Let righteous men be your dinner companions,
and let your glorying be in the fear of the Lord.

Ben Sira returns to the theme of 6:5-17, from the point of view of beginning a friendship. He prefers old friends to new; but if new are sought for, he mentions three classes to be excluded (vv. 11-13). (Last phrase in v. 13, read "and treading over a net.") Note in v. 15 how "the law of the Most High" is precisely what wise men will discuss. Verse 16, "dinner companions" suggests the Greek custom of the symposium, involving discussion, more or less serious, in the setting of a banquet.

## ON GOOD GOVERNMENT
9:17-10:5

17A work will be praised for the skill of the craftsmen;
so a people's leader is proved wise by his words.
18A babbler is feared in his city,
and the man who is reckless in speech will be hated.
**10** A wise magistrate will educate his people,
and the rule of an understanding
man will be well ordered.
2Like the magistrate of the people,
so are his officials;
and like the ruler of the city,
so are all its inhabitants.
3An undisciplined king will ruin his people,
but a city will grow through the
understanding of its rulers.
4The government of the earth is in the hands of the Lord,
and over it he will raise up the right man for the time.
5The success of a man is in the hands of the Lord,
and he confers his honor upon the person of the scribe.

In the Hellenistic age, roughly the last three centuries B.C., despite all the wars and rumors of wars, there was maintained in the schools of philosophy and in public opinion an ideal of the philanthropic and conscientious philosopher-king, who would strive sincerely and impartially to provide good and just government for his people. How often this ideal was realized is hard to say, but it certainly existed. Ben Sira here praises it, putting it in the perspective of his religious doctrine. He begins with the artisan/sage contrast (to be developed in 38:24-39:11): craftsmanship is important, indeed invaluable, but skill in government is the supreme social value, and that is possessed by the "wise magistrate." Ultimately, a competent and beneficent ruler is a gift from God. Verse 5b, "scribe" should be "commander" or "leader."

## ON ARROGANCE
10:6-18

6Do not be angry with your neighbor for any injury,
  and do not attempt anything by acts of insolence.
7Arrogance is hateful before the Lord and before men,
  and injustice is outrageous to both.
8Sovereignty passes from nation to nation
  on account of injustice and insolence and wealth.
9How can he who is dust and ashes be proud?
  for even in life his bowels decay.
10A long illness baffles the physician;
  the king of today will die tomorrow.
11For when a man is dead,
  he will inherit creeping things,
    and wild beasts, and worms.
12The beginning of man's pride is to depart from the Lord;
  his heart has forsaken his Maker.
13For the beginning of pride is sin,
  and the man who clings to it pours out abominations.
Therefore the Lord brought upon
  them extraordinary afflictions,
 and destroyed them utterly.
14The Lord has cast down the thrones of rulers,
  and has seated the lowly in their place.
15The Lord has plucked up the roots of the nations,
  and has planted the humble in their place.

> [16]The Lord has overthrown the lands of the nations,
>     and has destroyed them to the foundations of the earth.
> [17]He has removed some of them and destroyed them,
>     and has extinguished the memory of them from the
>     earth.
> [18]Pride was not created for men,
>     nor fierce anger for those born of women.

In five brief strophes Ben Sira denounces the capital sin of pride or arrogance. The Hebrew word is *ga'awah*, and it (or its verbal form) is repeated seven times. The Greek translator used as an equivalent the word *hubris*, familiar in Greek tragedy as an expression of human presumption which is infallibly punished by Fate. In the first strophe, vv. 6-8, loss of territory in war is seen as God's way of punishing an arrogant nation or monarch. Ben Sira must have witnessed such defeats often enough in his lifetime; most dramatically perhaps about 200 B.C. when Antiochus III of Syria wrested all of Palestine from the control of Ptolemy V of Egypt. In v. 9 the proverbial "dust and ashes" is used as an expression of the feebleness of man's physical make-up; cf. 17:32; Gen 18:27; Job 30:19. Ben Sira is fond of this reflection as a corrective to human pride. Verse 10 reminds us how abruptly any human life may be terminated, and v. 11 cites the humiliating corruption of the human body. ("Wild beasts" in RSV is a mistake; read "vermin.") This became a commonplace topic among moralizing historians who liked to picture the physical decay of the wicked beginning even before death. Cf. the lurid account of Antiochus IV's sufferings in 2 Mac 9:9f., and the death of Herod Agrippa in Acts 12:23. Verses 12-13 (third strophe): if fear of the Lord is the beginning of wisdom, the beginning of pride is the rejection of that fear. The 4th strophe (vv. 14-16) shows how the Lord punishes pride. In Mary's Canticle, Lk 1:52 is a summary quotation of v. 14. Verse 17, the only immortality known to Ben Sira was the continuance of a "name" on earth, either in children or in public remembrance. Lacking these, the deceased was completely extinct.

# TRUE HONOR
## 10:19-11:6

$^{19}$What race is worthy of honor?
  The human race.
 What race is worthy of honor?
  Those who fear the Lord.
What race is unworthy of honor?
  The human race.
 What race is unworthy of honor?
  Those who transgress the commandments.
$^{20}$Among brothers their leader is worthy of honor,
  and those who fear the Lord are worthy of honor in his
    eyes.
$^{22}$The rich, and the eminent, and the poor —
  their glory is the fear of the Lord.
$^{23}$It is not right to despise an intelligent poor man,
  nor is it proper to honor a sinful man.
$^{24}$The nobleman, and the judge,
  and the ruler will be honored,
 but none of them is greater
  than the man who fears the Lord.
$^{25}$Free men will be at the service of a wise servant,
  and a man of understanding will not grumble.
$^{26}$Do not make a display of your wisdom when you do
    your work,
  nor glorify yourself at a time when you are in want.
$^{27}$Better is a man who works and has an abundance of
    everything,
  than one who goes about boasting, but lacks bread.
$^{28}$My son, glorify yourself with humility,
  and ascribe to yourself honor
    according to your worth.
$^{29}$Who will justify the man that sins against himself?
  And who will honor the man
    that dishonors his own life?
$^{30}$A poor man is honored for his knowledge,
  while a rich man is honored for his wealth.

31A man honored in poverty, how
   much more in wealth!
 And a man dishonored in wealth,
   how much more in poverty!
**11**  The wisdom of a humble man
     will lift up his head,
   and will seat him among the great.
 2Do not praise a man for his good looks,
   nor loathe a man because of his appearance.
 3The bee is small among flying creatures,
   but her product is the best of sweet things.
 4Do not boast about wearing fine clothes,
   nor exalt yourself in the day that you are honored;
 for the works of the Lord are wonderful,
   and his works are concealed from men.
 5Many kings have had to sit on the ground,
   but one who was never thought of has worn a crown.
 6Many rulers have been greatly disgraced,
   and illustrious men have been handed over to others.

The theme of this section is the question of values in human life: in what does true glory or honor consist? Ben Sira firmly rejects external criteria such as social position, wealth, good looks, etc. A man's true value is from within and consists in his wisdom, prudence and fear of the Lord.

The opening verse is a fragment of dialogue exchanged between teacher and pupil. By its paradoxical form it invites the latter to reflect on the fundamental choice to be made by all humans. "Fear of the Lord" is here contrasted with "transgressing the commandments." In v. 22 and v. 24 various social classes are enumerated; in each case, the individual's worth is to be judged solely by his fear of the Lord. In v. 23 (and 11:1) we note that Ben Sira recognizes that a poor man may be wise; poverty therefore is not evidence of impiety or folly. Cf. Jas 2:1-7. Verse 25 echoes Prov 17:2, and is a surprisingly radical statement, if we consider the prevailing ideas about the inferiority, indeed subhuman character, of slaves. 26-27 contrast the snob who thinks manual labor beneath his dignity, with the man who is not ashamed to earn his living by it. This type of comparative proverb, "Better is A than B," was a favorite pedagogic device among the sages; *cf.* Prov 15:16f; Eccles 7:1-8. 28f. is a good example of Ben Sira's insight. In the previous section he had denounced pride; yet here he points out there may also be a false humility, that is, the crippling self-contempt that we call an inferiority complex. 30-31 point out that riches and poverty are not totally indifferent states: the former may add to a wise man's prestige and the latter may increase the ignominy of a fool. Finally, 11:2-6 warns against judging by appearance, or thinking that a present situation, good or bad, is not subject to change; the Lord, whose "works are concealed," is free to intervene at any moment.

## ON MODERATION
11:7-28

[7]Do not find fault before you investigate;
  first consider, and then reprove.
[8]Do not answer before you have heard,
  nor interrupt a speaker in the midst of his words.
[9]Do not argue about a matter
  which does not concern you,
 nor sit with sinners when they judge a case.
[10]My son, do not busy yourself with many matters;
  if you multiply activities you will not go unpunished,
  and if you pursue you will not escape.
[11]There is a man who works, and toils, and presses on,
  but is so much the more in want.
[12]There is another who is slow and needs help,
  who lacks strength and abounds in poverty;
but the eyes of the Lord looks upon him for his good;
  he lifts him out of his low estate
[13]and raises up his head,
  so that many are amazed at him.
[14]Good things and bad, life and death,
  poverty and wealth, come from the Lord.

17The gift of the Lord endures for those who are godly,
and what he approves will have lasting success.
18There is a man who is rich through
his diligence and self-denial,
and this is the reward allotted to him:
19when he says, "I have found rest,
and now I shall enjoy my goods!"
he does not know how much time will pass
until he leaves them to others and dies.
20Stand by your covenant and attend to it,
and grow old in your work.
21Do not wonder at the works of a sinner,
but trust in the Lord and keep at your toil;
for it is easy in the sight of the Lord
to enrich a poor man quickly and suddenly.
22The blessing of the Lord is the reward of the godly,
and quickly God causes his blessing to flourish.
23Do not say, "What do I need,
and what prosperity could be mine in the future?"
24Do not say, "I have enough,
and what calamity could happen to me in the future?"
25In the day of prosperity, adversity is forgotten,
and in the day of adversity,
prosperity is not remembered.
26For it is easy in the sight of the Lord
to reward a man on the day of death
according to his conduct.
27The misery of an hour makes one forget luxury,
and at the close of a man's life
his deeds will be revealed.
28Call no one happy before his death;
a man will be known through his children.

As a follow-up to the preceding sections, against pride and against superficial judgements, Ben Sira now considers the golden mean, the middle way between two extremes. This is his version of the Greek slogan, *meden agan,* "Nothing too much." There are some interesting parallels here with his predecessor Qoheleth.

The Sage begins (vv. 7-9) by condemning premature judgments, as also involvement in others' business (v. 8, cf. Prov 18:13). Then, with renewed address "My son," he warns (vv. 10-13) against being a "workaholic" in pursuit of wealth. As always, Ben Sira insists that human beings must not "play God"; they must act, of course, as prudently and effectively as they can, but realizing always that the last word belongs to the Lord. Cf. Prov 10:22, 16:9, etc.; Eccles 4:8, 6: 2. Ben Sira expresses reverent amazement (v. 13) at the Lord's actions in reversing human fortunes (as in vv. 4-6, 12); he does not suggest that such reverses can be explained as reward or punishment for human acts.

Verse 14 brings a favorite doctrine of Ben Sira: the universal causality of the God of Israel. All dualism is excluded from this sapiential theology. There is not — as there was in Zoroastrianism, for example — any evil Spirit on a level with the Lord, to whom things wrong or evil or displeasing might be attributed. Unflinchingly Ben Sira affirms the origin in the Lord of evil as well as good, death as well as life, etc., leaving for later discussion how this is to be understood. Cf. below 15:11-20, 39:25ff., and cf. Isa 45:7. RSV rightly puts vv. 15-16 in a footnote; they are a gloss by some early editor who wished to make the distinction that Ben Sira rejected:

> [15]Wisdom, understanding, and knowledge of the law come from the Lord; affection and the ways of good works come from him. [16]Error and darkness were created with sinners; evil will grow old with those who take pride in malice.

In vv. 17-19 the "reward allotted" is of course meant ironically; Ben Sira is still insisting that "man proposes but God disposes." 18-19 is expanded in dramatic dialogue form in the Lucan parable, Lk 12:16-21. With v. 20 Ben Sira returns to direct address (Hebrew reads "My son") and refers to "task" and "work." These may be understood as one's daily work, but perhaps better, one's religious duties in the service of God, "covenant" in RSV. Verse 21ab is an admonition, often repeated elsewhere, against being envious of the wicked who are prosperous; cf. Prov 3:31, 24:1, 19; Ps 37:1, 73:3. The fact was obviously a scandal to many in Israel. Verse 22 is a reassurance — cautiously expressed by Ben Sira, who wrote "in due time"; the translator substituted "quickly." Verses 23-24 are quotations (as in 5:1-6 and 7:9) of what a person might secretly think: v. 23 is the pessimist's view, "I can never be happy," v. 24 the optimist's, "No evil can touch me." Ben Sira reminds them both that the Lord may punish or reward at any time, and previous joy or sorrow will then be forgotten (v. 25). He is not thinking of any happiness after death, but he believes that happiness or the reverse in the hour of death is of supreme importance. If a person dies happy, that shows that his or her deeds were pleasing to the Lord. Verse 28, RSV follows the Greek; but Ben Sira wrote, "...known by how his life ends."

## THE CHOICE OF FRIENDS
11:29-13:1

$^{29}$Do not bring every man into your home,
   for many are the wiles of the crafty.
$^{30}$Like a decoy partridge in a cage,
   so is the mind of a proud man,
   and like a spy he observes your weakness;
$^{31}$For he lies in wait, turning good into evil,
   and to worthy actions he will attach blame.
$^{32}$From a spark of fire come many burning coals,
   and a sinner lies in wait to shed blood.
$^{33}$Beward of a scoundrel, for he devises evil,
   lest he give you a lasting blemish.
$^{34}$Receive a stranger into your home
   and he will upset you with commotion,
    and will estrange you from your family.
**12** If you do a kindness, know to whom you do it,
   and you will be thanked for your good deeds.

2Do good to a godly man, and you will be repaid —
   if not by him, certainly by the Most High.
3No good will come to the man who persists in evil
   or to him who does not give alms.
4Give to the godly man, but do not help the sinner.
   5Do good to the humble, but do not give to the
      ungodly;
hold back his bread, and do not give it to him,
   lest by means of it he subdue you;
for you will receive twice as much evil
   for all the good which you do to him.
6For the Most High also hates sinners
   and will inflict punishment on the ungodly.
7Give to the good man, but do not help the sinner.
8A friend will not be known in prosperity,
   nor will an enemy be hidden in adversity.
9A man's enemies are grieved when he prospers,
   and in his adversity even his friend will separate from
   him.
10Never trust your enemy,
   for like the rusting of copper, so is his wickedness.
11Even if he humbles himself and goes about cringing,
   watch yourself, and be on your guard against him;
and you will be to him like one
   who has polished a mirror,
   and you will know that it was
   not hopelessly tarnished.
12Do not put him next to you,
   lest he overthrow you and take your place;
do not have him sit at your right,
   lest he try to take your seat of honor,
and at last you will realize the truth of my words,
   and be stung by what I have said.
13Who will pity a snake charmer bitten by a serpent,
   or any who go near wild beasts?
14So no one will pity a man who associates with a sinner
   and becomes involved in his sins.
15He will stay with you for a time,
   but if you falter, he will not stand by you.

16An enemy will speak sweetly with his lips.
  but in his mind he will plan to throw you
    into a pit;
an enemy will weep with his eyes,
  but if he finds an opportunity
    his thirst for blood will be insatiable.
17If calamity befalls you, you will
  find him there ahead of you;
 and while pretending to help you,
  he will trip you by the heel;
18he will shake his head, and clap his hands,
  and whisper much, and change his expression.
**13**  Whoever touches pitch will be defiled,
  and whoever associates with a proud man will
    become like him.

Since it is so difficult to determine a person's true character in a short acquaintance, Ben Sira recommends great caution in the choice of friends. A first section (11:29-34) lists five bad characters who will cause nothing but trouble: the crafty, proud, sinner, scoundrel, stranger. In the next section, 12:1-7, Ben Sira analyzes a tricky problem in casuistry. With the best of intentions it is possible for someone to become involved with impious or dishonest people, by aiding them with gifts or in deeds. Discrimination is very necessary. Verse 1 sets the tone; then in a series of antitheses — godly/evil, good/sinner, humble/ungodly — Ben Sira makes his point. Help to the first member of each pair is virtuous and worthy of reward; given to the others, it will have only bad effects, for other people and for the giver.

Skip v. 7 as a doublet of v. 4. Verse 8, the point is that everybody seems friendly to the prosperous person, but in adversity those who were secretly hostile will be revealed. In 12:8-13:1 Ben Sira develops a series of contrasts in sapiential style. Friends and enemies are two fixed classes; we are not told how they got that way, nor whether it is possible to pass from one class to the other. The enemies of course are wicked, whereas Ben Sira's auditors are and will always continue to be honest, virtuous and Godfearing. Despite the chapter division, 13:1 is a summary of what precedes — cp. 12:14.

## INCOMPATIBILITY OF RICH AND POOR
## 13:2-24

2Do not lift a weight beyond your strength,
nor associate with a man mightier and richer than you.
How can the clay pot associate with the iron kettle?
The pot will strike against it,
and will itself be broken.
3A rich man does wrong, and he even adds reproaches;
a poor man suffers wrong, and he must add apologies.
4A rich man will exploit you if you can be of use to him,
but if you are in need he will forsake you.
5If you own something, he will live with you;
he will drain your resources and he will not care.
6When he needs you he will deceive you,
he will smile at you and give you hope.
He will speak to you kindly and say, "What do you need?"
7He will shame you with his foods,
until he has drained you two or three times;
and finally he will deride you.
Should he see you afterwards, he will forsake you,
and shake his head at you.
8Take care not to be led astray,
and not to be humiliated in your feasting.
9When a powerful man invites you, be reserved;
and he will invite you the more often.
10Do not push forward, lest you be repulsed;
and do not remain at a distance,
lest you be forgotten.
11Do not try to treat him as an equal,
nor trust his abundance of words;
for he will test you through much talk,
and while he smiles he will be examining you.
12Cruel is he who does not keep words to himself;
he will not hesitate to injure or to imprison.
13Keep words to yourself and be very watchful,
for you are walking about with your own downfall.

[15]Every creature loves its like,
  and every person his neighbor;
[16]all living beings associate by species,
  and a man clings to one like himself.
[17]What fellowship has a wolf with a lamb?
  No more has a sinner with a godly man.
[18]What peace is there between a hyena and a dog?
  And what peace between a rich man and a poor man?
[19]Wild asses in the wilderness are the prey of lions;
  likewise the poor are pastures for the rich.
[20]Humility is an abomination to a proud man;
  likewise a poor man is an abomination to a rich one.
[21]When a rich man totters, he is steadied by friends,
  but when a humble man falls, he
    is even pushed away by friends.
[22]If a rich man slips, his helpers are many;
  he speaks unseemly words, and they justify him.
If a humble man slips, they even reproach him;
  he speaks sensibly, and receives no attention.
[23]When the rich man speaks all are silent,
  and they extol to the clouds what he says.
When the poor man speaks they say, "Who is this
  fellow?"
  And should he stumble, they even push him down.
[24]Riches are good if they are free from sin,
  and poverty is evil in the opinion of the ungodly.

This is the first long section in which there is no mention of God, and scarcely any of religious values (only vv. 17 and 24). Ben Sira here speaks as a man of the world, cold-bloodedly appraising the realities of wealth and political power, and giving shrewd Machiavellian advice to young men who will soon find themselves at grips with those realities. If that is a fair statement of the case, he would not be the last "man of God" to show himself more than a match for worldly intriguers at their own game. Is this perhaps what Jesus meant by being "wise as serpents" (Mt 10:16)?

After what we observed about the apparent wealth or at least financial security of Ben Sira's auditors (4:1-10), it comes as a surprise to find him putting them in the class of the poor, liable to vexation and oppression on the part of the rich. All such classification, of course, is relative; as almsgivers, they might be moderately well off, while still far from the category of millionaires.

A first sub-section is 13:2-8, on the contrast of poor and rich. The comparison in v. 2cd is found in Aesop's Fables, and no doubt was widely known. In v. 3 the contrast is extreme, and satirical. Verse 7, the head-shaking indicates mockery. 9-13 continues in the same vein, but now it is "a powerful man," lit. "prince," "nobleman," who is the predominant and oppressive partner. Ben Sira coolly indicates (vv. 10-11) the appropriate attitude to take. 13b, read "do not go about with violent men." 15-20 generalizes, with images again reminiscent of Aesop: wolf/lamb, hyena/dog, wild ass/lion. The judgment implied seems rather harsh, if applied to all and any rich people; but "sinner" in v. 17 suggests that Ben Sira has in mind some specific group who were not only wealthy but impious apostates. The last two strophes, vv. 21-22, vv. 23-24, develop in satirical and humorous style the contrast established back in v. 3. 22d, this brushing aside of the wise but poor was already recorded in Eccles 9:13-16. 24 sums up in balanced terms Ben Sira's teaching.

## TRUE HAPPINESS
13:25-14:2

> $^{25}$A man's heart changes his countenance,
> either for good or for evil.
> $^{26}$The mark of a happy heart is a cheerful face,
> but to devise proverbs requires painful thinking.
> **14** Blessed is the man who does not blunder with his lips
> and need not suffer grief for sin.
> $^{2}$Blessed is he whose heart does not condemn him,
> and who has not given up his hope.

This little piece is a reflection on true happiness, which essentially consists in a clear conscience ("heart"). This is neatly affirmed in the two beatitudes, a favorite sapiential form. 26b should read "solitude and worry (cause) painful thinking."

## WRONG AND RIGHT USE OF WEALTH
## 14:3-19

[3]Riches are not seemly for a stingy man;
   and of what use is property to an envious man?
[4]Whoever accumulates by depriving himself,
      accumulates for others;
   and others will live in luxury on his goods.
[5]If a man is mean to himself,
   to whom will he be generous?
   He will not enjoy his own riches.
[6]No one is meaner than the man who is grudging to
      himself,
   and this is the retribution for his baseness;
[7]even if he does good, he does it unintentionally,
   and betrays his baseness in the end.
[8]Evil is the man with a grudging eye;
   he averts his face and disregards people.
[9]A greedy man's eye is not satisfied with a portion,
   and mean injustice withers the soul.
[10]A stingy man's eye begrudges bread,
   and it is lacking at his table.
[11]My son, treat yourself well,
      according to your means,
   and present worthy offerings to the Lord.
[12]Remember that death will not delay,
   and the decree of Hades has not been shown to you.
[13]Do good to a friend before you die,
   and reach out and give to him as much as you can.
[14]Do not deprive yourself of a happy day;
   let not your share of desired good pass by you.
[15]Will you not leave the fruit of your labors to another,
   and what you acquired by toil to be divided by lot?
[16]Give, and take, and beguile yourself,
   because in Hades one cannot look for luxury.

17All living beings become old like a garment,
   for the decree from of old is,
     "You must surely die!"
18Like flourishing leaves on a spreading tree
   which sheds some and puts forth others,
so are the generations of flesh and blood:
   one dies and another is born.
19Every product decays and ceases to exist,
   and the man who made it will pass away with it.

Ben Sira believed that money was to be used, not hoarded — for the owner's benefit and enjoyment, but also for his family and friends. In spite of his censures of the rich in the previous chapter he supposes that his pupils will at least be in a position to enjoy the good things of this world. These are God's gifts, to be enjoyed gratefully and with moderation. Naturally he has no doctrine of religious asceticism, no idea of "giving up" anything in view of a happy future life. In this he is fully in accord with his predecessor Ecclesiastes. At the same time he is no Epicurean. We may remember that the faithful observance of the Mosaic law already required and imposed considerable restraint and self-denial, in the midst of a Gentile world.

Verses 3-10 deal first with the miser; "stingy man" is lit. "little heart," making a word link with "heart" in the preceding section. "Envious man" is lit. "man of the evil eye," a link with "eye" in 8-10. Verse 4 echoes Eccles 2:21, 6:2. Verses 11-16 then treat of the right use and enjoyment of money, set off against the dark prevision of the finality of death. 15 is an explicit reminder that "you can't take it with you." Cf. Eccles 2:24, 3:13, 5:17f., 8:15, 9:7-10. Finally, vv. 17-19 focus on the underlying motif of human mortality. The "decree" may be an express allusion to the Paradise story, Gen 2:17, 3:19; cf. below, 25:24. Verse 18 is a paraphrase of a famous quotation from Homer, Iliad 6, 146: "As are the generations of leaves, so are those of men."

# IV

## THE PURSUIT AND ATTAINMENT OF WISDOM
14:20-15:10

$^{20}$Blessed is the man who meditates on wisdom
and who reasons intelligently.
$^{21}$He who reflects in his mind on her ways
will also ponder her secrets.
$^{22}$Pursue wisdom like a hunter,
and lie in wait on her paths.
$^{23}$He who peers through her windows
will also listen at her doors;
$^{24}$he who encamps near her house
will also fasten his tent peg to her walls;
$^{25}$he will pitch his tent near her,
and will lodge in an excellent lodging place;
$^{26}$he will place his children under her shelter,
and will camp under her boughs;
$^{27}$he will be sheltered by her from the heat,
and will dwell in the midst of her glory.
**15** The man who fears the Lord will do this,
and he who holds to the law will obtain wisdom.
$^2$She will come to meet him like a mother,
and like the wife of his youth she will welcome him.
$^3$She will feed him with the bread of understanding,
and give him the water of wisdom to drink.

70

⁴He will lean on her and will not fall,
 and he will rely on her and will not be put to shame.
⁵She will exalt him above his neighbors,
 and will open his mouth in the midst of the assembly.
⁶He will find gladness and a crown of rejoicing,
 and will acquire an everlasting name.
⁷Foolish men will not obtain her,
 and sinful men will not see her.
⁸She is far from men of pride,
 and liars will never think of her.
⁹A hymn of praise is not fitting on the lips of a sinner,
 for it has not been sent from the Lord.
¹⁰For a hymn of praise should be uttered in wisdom,
 and the Lord will prosper it.

This passage is the fourth of Ben Sira's praises of Wisdom, again personified as mother and spouse. The first sub-section, 14:20-15:1, begins with a beatitude; then in a picturesque series of relative clauses it develops the metaphor of the hunter, patiently stalking Wisdom till he can get a good shot. In v. 23 he changes into a "peeping Tom," then (v. 26) into a bird. "Children" is a mistake; read "He will build his nest in her foliage, and will lodge in her branches." 15:1 is a highly condensed summary: "fears the Lord" = "holds to the law" = "obtain wisdom." For Ben Sira these three are inseparable. In the second sub-section, 15:2-10, all this activity pays off, when the quarry pursued comes to meet the pursuer, in the familiar human guise of Lady Wisdom. The theme of food and drink (v. 3) harks back to Wisdom's banquet in Prov 9:1ff. Verses 4-6 in plain terms set out her benefits; 7-8 list four categories of men (opposed to those of v. 1) who cannot attain her.

## ON FREE WILL
15:11-20

¹¹Do not say, "Because of the Lord
 I left the right way";
 for he will not do what he hates.

$^{12}$Do not say, "It was he who led me astray";
  for he has no need of a sinful man.
$^{13}$The Lord hates all abominations,
  and they are not loved by those who fear him.
$^{14}$It was he who created man in the beginning,
  and he left him in the power of his own inclination.
$^{15}$If you will, you can keep the commandments,
  and to act faithfully is a matter of your own choice.
$^{16}$He has placed before you fire and water:
  stretch out your hand for whichever you wish.
$^{17}$Before a man are life and death,
  and whichever he chooses will be given to him.
$^{18}$For great is the wisdom of the Lord;
  he is mighty in power and sees everything;
$^{19}$his eyes are on those who fear him,
  and he knows every deed of man.
$^{20}$He has not commanded any one to be ungodly,
  and he has not given any one permission to sin.

Ben Sira here tackles a notorious problem, that of reconciling genuine human liberty and responsibility, with the over-riding and all-powerful will of God. He deals with it, one may say, in stages; here, he strenuously defends liberty; later (18:1-13, 33:13-15) he will dwell on God's supremacy and rule. Whether he has managed really to reconcile them may be doubted; but then, who has?

Beginning with two dramatic quotations, vv. 11-13 seem to be rebutting the argument that, since God is the cause of every act, he must also be the cause of human sin. The rebuttal is repeated in NT, Jas 1:13f. Verse 14a uses the technical vocabulary of Gen 1:1, 27; "man" is here *ha'adam*, a collective noun meaning "the human race." Verse 14b is the key statement; lit., "set him in the power of his (own) *yeser*." Later rabbis distinguished a good *yeser* (virtuous inclination) from an evil one (sinful inclination). But Ben Sira here seems to use the word in a neutral sense, practically = free will. The argument then is that the good Creator created humankind good, endowed with a faculty of choice also good, because really free; but, because really free, also capable of a wrong and evil choice. If that capability is actuated, its evil cannot be ascribed to the one who created the faculty good and free.

Verses 15-17 dispassionately underline human responsibility for the morality of one's actions. 15a, "commandments" is probably a general reference to that morality, rather than to the particular ten. 17 borrows its image from Deut 30:15, 19, cf. Jer 21:8. 18-19 eloquently insist on the Lord's all-seeing eyes — cf. Ps 33:13-19, esp. v. 18a which Ben Sira here quotes. Verse 20 sums up, referring back to vv. 11-13.

## PUNISHMENT FOR SIN
16:1-23

**16** Do not desire a multitude of useless children,
nor rejoice in ungodly sons.
²If they multiply, do not rejoice in them,
unless the fear of the Lord is in them.
³Do not trust in their survival,
and do not rely on their multitude;
for one is better than a thousand,
and to die childless is better
than to have ungodly children.
⁴For through one man of understanding a city will be
filled with people,
but through a tribe of lawless
men it will be made desolate.
⁵Many such things my eye has seen,
and my ear has heard things more striking than these.
⁶In an assembly of sinners a fire will be kindled,
and in a disobedient nation wrath was kindled.
⁷He was not propitiated for the ancient giants
who revolted in their might.
⁸He did not spare the neighbors of Lot,
whom he loathed on account of their insolence.
⁹He showed no pity for a nation devoted to destruction,
for those destroyed in their sins;

$^{10}$nor for the six hundred thousand men on foot,
   who rebelliously assembled in their stubbornness.
$^{11}$Even if there is only one stiff-necked person,
   it will be a wonder if he remains unpunished.
For mercy and wrath are with the Lord;
   he is mighty to forgive, and he pours out wrath.
$^{12}$As great as his mercy, so great is also his reproof;
   he judges a man according to his deeds.
$^{13}$The sinner will not escape with his plunder,
   and the patience of the godly will not be frustrated.
$^{14}$He will make room for every act of mercy;
   every one will receive in accordance with his deeds.
$^{17}$Do not say, "I shall be hidden from the Lord,
   and who from on high will remember me?
Among so many people I shall not be known,
   for what is my soul in the boundless creation?
$^{18}$Behold, heaven and the highest heaven,
   the abyss and the earth, will tremble at his visitation.
$^{19}$The mountains also and the foundations of the earth
   shake with trembling when he looks upon them.
$^{20}$And no mind will reflect on this.
   Who will ponder his ways?
$^{21}$Like a tempest which no man can see,
   so most of his works are concealed.
$^{22}$Who will announce his acts of justice?
   Or who will await them? For the covenant is far off."
$^{23}$This is what one devoid of understanding thinks;
   a senseless and misguided man thinks foolishly.

A numerous family, especially of boys, was proverbially considered to be one of the greatest blessings a man could ask or receive from the Lord. But Ben Sira adds a rider: *provided* they be obedient and God-fearing. Otherwise, many children may be more of a curse than a blessing. One may suspect a real "case" behind this little passage, vv. 1-5; a Jewish apostate, whom Ben Sira would consider wicked and ungodly, may have argued, "I have a large family; that proves I have God's approval and am not a sinner." Ben Sira retorts as in v. 3. A similar judgment is voiced in the later

Wis 4:3-6. Verse 5 makes a transition: Ben Sira has observed unfaithful families: he has also heard of (i.e. read about) impious groups in Israelite history, which he proceeds to enumerate in the following unit, vv. 6-11b. This v. 5 is one of several places where Ben Sira steps forward to refer to his personal experiences; such "individualism" was new in Hebrew writing and no doubt was due to hellenistic influence and example.

The second unit, vv. 6-11b, lists five groups of impious rebels whose destruction for their wickedness was narrated in the sacred books Ben Sira had studied. 6, the "sinners" were the followers of Korah (Num 16). 7, "giants" refers to the antediluvian "men of renown," Gen 6:4. 8, the "neighbors of Lot" are the citizens of Sodom, Gen 19:4-11. 9, the "nation" is that of the Canaanites, who according to the tradition were exterminated by the Lord before the invading tribes of Israel, cf. e.g. Deut 7:1ff. 10 refers to those rebellious Israelites who died in the course of the desert wandering: cf. Ex 12:37 + Num 14:22f.

The third unit, vv. 11c-14, begins with a repetition of 5:6; it insists on God's anger against the impenitent, combined with ready mercy for the repentant and reward for the doers of good. The last two units, vv. 17-19 and vv. 20-23, condemn the sceptic who feels that the Almighty has so much to attend to that one individual sinner may hope to escape his notice altogether and sin with impunity. In v. 23 Ben Sira brushes this argumentation aside with a brief condemnation. He will handle it somewhat more at length in 17:15-24 and 23:19-20.

# V

## DIVINE GOVERNMENT OF THE UNIVERSE AND OF MANKIND
### 16:24-18:14

### Creation of Sky and Earth
### 16:24-30

$^{24}$Listen to me, my son, and acquire knowledge,
and pay close attention to my words.
$^{25}$I will impart instruction by weight,
and declare knowledge accurately.
$^{26}$The works of the Lord have existed from the beginning
by his creation.
and when he made them, he determined their divisions.
$^{27}$He arranged his works in an eternal order,
and their dominion for all generations;
they neither hunger nor grow weary,
and they do not cease from their labors.
$^{28}$They do not crowd one another aside,
and they will never disobey his word.
$^{29}$After this the Lord looked upon the earth,
and filled it with his good things;
$^{30}$with all kinds of living beings he covered its surface,
and to it they return.

This is the first of Ben Sira's three great compositions on God as Creator and Governor of the universe (the others,

39:12-35, 42:15-43:35). They are poetic commentaries on the opening chapters of Genesis, which obviously he had studied carefully and meditated on lovingly. His own doctrinal reflections and expansions of the material are penetrating and enriching.

The first unit is 16:24-30, dealing with heavenly bodies and the earth. 24-25 are a solemn introduction, inviting the student's close attention to instruction and knowledge. Ben Sira sets a remarkable example, as a firm believer who wishes to combine the traditional doctrine of creation with the best scientific knowledge of his day. There is no trace here of obscurantism or fundamentalism. He is thoroughly positive and optimistic in his approach to the physical sciences — also, as we shall see, to history. The first "works" considered, in vv. 26-28, are clearly the sun, moon and stars. Ben Sira is impressed not so much by their existence as by the never-failing regularity of their movements, which govern the successions of day and night, of seasons and of years. These are "their labors." Verses 29-30 summarize the rest of Gen 1, down to the creation of land animals. In v. 29b "good things" is an echo of the repeated "God saw that it was good." In v. 30b, the "return" of living things to the earth is not mentioned in Gen 1 but comes from Ps 104:29.

## Creation of the Human Race
## 17:1-10

**17** The Lord created man out of earth,
and turned him back to it again.
²He gave to men few days, a limited time,
but granted them authority over the things upon the
earth.
³He endowed them with strength like his own,
and made them in his own image.
⁴He placed the fear of them in all living beings,
and granted them dominion over beasts and birds.
⁶He made for them tongue and eyes;
he gave them ears and a mind for thinking.
⁷He filled them with knowledge and understanding,
and showed them good and evil.

8He set his eye upon their hearts
  to show them the majesty of his works.
10And they will praise his holy name,
  to proclaim the grandeur of his works.

## Election of Israel
## 17:11-20

11He bestowed knowledge upon them,
  and allotted to them the law of life.
12He established with them an eternal covenant,
  and showed them his judgments.
13Their eyes saw his glorious majesty,
  and their ears heard the glory of his voice.
14And he said to them, "Beware of all unrighteousness."
  And he gave commandment to each of them concern-
    ing his neighbor.
15Their ways are always before him,
  they will not be hid from his eyes.
17He appointed a ruler for every nation,
  but Israel is the Lord's own portion.
19All their works are as the sun before him,
  and his eyes are continually upon their ways.
20Their iniquities are not hidden from him,
  and all their sins are before the Lord.

Verses 17:1-20 cover the creation of humankind, the election of Israel, and the consequences of both these divine
acts. The first is described in vv. 1-10 (NAB translates vv.
2-10 in the present tense, but RSV's historic style is preferable); Ben Sira weaves together details from the different
narratives of Gen 1 and 2-3. For instance, in v. 1 "created
man" comes from Gen 1:27, but the rest of the verse is from
Gen 2:7 and 3:19. Verse 7 is important: it pictures God as
already imparting the great gift of wisdom to the first
humans, and, in parallel with that, showing them good and
evil. This is a noteworthy and probably correct interpretation of the "tree of knowledge" of Gen 2:9, 17; 3:5, 22. To
"know" for the Israelite was not simply to receive an impression or information; it was an action which affected the
thing known. To "know" good and evil was to determine for

oneself what one judged to be conducive and desirable, or the opposite. By forbidding the tree's fruit to the humans the Lord God declared that he knew the eating of it to be evil *for them*. By rejecting that knowledge, Man and Woman substituted their own, and "knew" the tree's fruit as good — for them. Gen 3:22a is not ironical, as some would have it. It is a simple recognition of the fact that the humans have become "like gods" because they have acted like gods; they have tried to "know," i.e. determine, good and evil.

The section following, vv. 11-20, deals with the election of Israel; v. 17, which is certainly out of place, should probably go at the beginning, between vv. 10 and 11. 17a, the "ruler" envisaged is not an earthly king (as in 10:4) but a sort of heavenly viceroy, what we would call a patron or guardian angel. The idea is that since Israel has a unique relationship to the Lord, by virtue of the Sinai covenant, he attends to her government in person and delegates to others the government of other nations. Cf. Deut 32:8f.; Dan 10:13, 20f. 11-12, "law," "covenant," "judgments" are all words associated with the covenant-making at Sinai. 13 alludes to the theophany described in such majestic terms in Ex 19:16-20, 24:9-11. 14 is Ben Sira's attempt at "the two greatest commandments": the first is the most general possible ethical principle, the second is substantially the same as Jesus' choice, "Thou shalt love thy neighbor as thyself." Verses 15, 19-20, correcting 16:17-22, insist again on God's surveillance of the moral behavior of each member of his people.

## The Moral Law and God's Mercy
17:22-32

22A man's almsgiving is like a signet with the Lord,
   and he will keep a person's
      kindness like the apple of his eye.
23Afterward he will arise and requite them,
   and he will bring their recompense on their heads.
24Yet to those who repent he grants a return,
   and he encourages those whose endurance is failing.
25Turn to the Lord and forsake your sins;
   pray in his presence and lessen your offenses.

$^{26}$Return to the Most High and turn away from iniquity,
   and hate abominations intensely.
$^{27}$Who will sing praises to the Most High in Hades,
   as do those who are alive and give thanks?
$^{28}$From the dead, as from one who does not exist, thanks-
      giving has ceased;
   he who is alive and well sings the Lord's praises.
$^{29}$How great is the mercy of the Lord,
   and his forgiveness for those who turn to him!
$^{30}$For all things cannot be in men,
   since a son of man is not immortal.
$^{31}$What is brighter than the sun? Yet its light fails.
   So flesh and blood devise evil.
$^{32}$He marshals the host of the height of heaven;
   but all men are dust and ashes.

17:22-24 is a transition passage, between the Lord's scru-
tiny of human acts (vv. 19-20) and the following summons to
repentance (vv. 25-32). It makes three points: the Lord loves
the righteous; he will punish the unrepentant; he welcomes
the penitent. The latter, as an individual, is directly
addressed in vv. 25f. Repentance glorifies the Lord (v. 28b),
therefore it should be practised before one descends to
Sheol (Hades), where there is neither prayer nor praise.
Again we see that Ben Sira's conservative theology does not
permit him to accept the newer doctrine of a judgment after
death and resurrection of the just, as expressed later in Dan
12:2-3. Verses 30-32 are a slightly confused reflection on
human insufficiency, expressed in two standard images.

God's Power and Compassion
18:1-14
   **18**   He who lives for ever created the whole
      universe;
   $^2$the Lord alone will be declared righteous.
$^4$To none has he given power to proclaim his works;
   and who can search out his mighty deeds?
$^5$Who can measure his majestic power?
   And who can fully recount his mercies?

⁶It is not possible to diminish or increase them,
  nor is it possible to trace the wonders of the Lord.
⁷When a man has finished, he is just beginning,
  and when he stops, he will be at a loss.
⁸What is man, and of what use is he?
  What is his good and what is his evil?
⁹The number of a man's days is great if he reaches a
    hundred years.
¹⁰Like a drop of water from the sea and a grain of sand
  so are a few years in the day of eternity.
¹¹Therefore the Lord is patient with them
  and pours out his mercy upon them.
¹²He sees and recognizes that their end will be evil;
  therefore he grants them forgiveness in abundance.
¹³The compassion of man is for his neighbor,
  but the compassion of the Lord is for all living beings.
He rebukes and trains and teaches them,
  and turns them back, as a shepherd his flock.
¹⁴He has compassion on those who accept his discipline
  and who are eager for his judgments.

In the concluding section of this great rhapsody, 18:1-14, Ben Sira marvels at God's power (vv. 1-7), contrasts man's insignificance (vv. 8-10), and praises God's mercy (vv. 11-14). Verse 1: it may be of interest to note that St. Augustine's Old Latin version read ". . . created all things at the same time." This led Augustine to declare that the six-day process described in Gen 1 was obviously an artificial pedagogic device to cover, as it were, all corners of the universe, but not to be taken as a literal week. Would that subsequent scholars had accepted Augustine's insight, in interpreting symbolically the creation account in Gen 1:1—2:4a! . . . In vv. 4-7 Ben Sira gives eloquent expression to his profound and reverent awe before the mysteries of God's creative work. Verses 8-10 make a strong contrast with 17:1-10, where a series of marvelous divine gifts was considered; here it is the pettiness and brevity of human existence in itself that are presented. Cp. a similar contrast in Ps 8, which Ben Sira is here quoting. In v. 10 he quotes himself, 1:2 above. The last strophe of all, vv. 11-14, brings a consoling idea, most beautifully expressed. So far from being impatient or severe with such feeble creatures, the Lord finds in their ephemeral nature a motive for pity and compassion. Verse 13ab is another pithy epigram, and the shepherd image adds a touch of intimacy. Ben Sira seems here to have in mind the whole human race, yet v. 14 seems to narrow down the reference to Jews and proselytes; it may be an editor's gloss.

## KIND AND PRUDENT SPEECH
18:15-29

[15]My son, do not mix reproach with your good deeds,
  nor cause grief by your words when you present a gift.
[17]Indeed, does not a word surpass a good gift?
  Both are to be found in a gracious man.
[18]A fool is ungracious and abusive,
  and the gift of a grudging man makes the eyes dim.
[19]Before you speak, learn,
  and before you fall ill, take care of your health.
[20]Before judgment, examine yourself,
  and in the hour of visitation you will find forgiveness.
[21]Before falling ill, humble yourself,
  and when you are on the point of sinning, turn back.
[22]Let nothing hinder you from paying a vow promptly,
  and do not wait until death to be released from it.
[23]Before making a vow, prepare yourself;
  and do not be like a man who tempts the Lord.
[24]Think of his wrath on the day of death,
  and of the moment of vengeance when he turns away
    his face.
[25]In the time of plenty think of the time of hunger;
  in the days of wealth think of poverty and need.
[26]From morning to evening conditions change,
  and all things move swiftly before the Lord.
[27]A wise man is cautious in everything,
  and in days of sin he guards against wrongdoing.
[28]Every intelligent man knows wisdom,
  and he praises the one who finds her.

29Those who understand sayings
　　become skilled themselves,
　　and pour forth apt proverbs.

We return now to workaday maxims of prudent behavior. In vv. 15-18 there is a good example of Ben Sira's psychological insight: how a gift may be ruined by tactless speech. 19-21 inculcate foresight in personal matters. 22-25, the same, with regard to making vows, i.e. promises to offer sacrifices if prayers are answered. Ben Sira here fully agrees with Eccles 5:2-6. 26-29 concern the wise man, especially in his duty of popularizing wisdom. This emphasis illustrates the zeal ascribed to Ben Sira in the Prologue by his grandson, and the grandson's own diligence.

## ON SELF-CONTROL
18:30-19:4

30Do not follow your base desires,
　　but restrain your appetites.
31If you allow your soul to take pleasure in base desire,
　　it will make you the laughingstock of your enemies.
32Do not revel in great luxury,
　　lest you become impoverished by its expense.
33Do not become a beggar by feasting with borrowed money,
　　when you have nothing in your purse.
**19**　A workman who is a drunkard will not become rich;
　　he who despises small things will fail little by little.
2Wine and women lead intelligent men astray,
　　and the man who consorts with harlots is very reckless.
3Decay and worms will inherit him,
　　and the reckless soul will be snatched away.
4One who trusts others too quickly is lightminded,
　　and one who sins does wrong to himself.

These rather miscellaneous warnings are in standard sapiential terms: the threatened consequences are this-worldly, down-to-earth results, such as mockery, poverty, disease, even premature death. The vices censured are lust, gluttony and squandering of money. The whole is an outline of the experience of the Prodigal Son (Lk 15:11-32).

## THE PROPER USE OF SPEECH
19:5-17

$^5$One who rejoices in wickedness will be condemned,
$^6$ and for one who hates gossip evil is lessened.
$^7$Never repeat a conversation,
   and you will lose nothing at all.
$^8$With friend or foe do not report it,
   and unless it would be a sin for you,
      do not disclose it;
$^9$for some one has heard you and watched you,
   and when the time comes he will hate you.
$^{10}$Have you heard a word? Let it die with you.
   Be brave! It will not make you burst!
$^{11}$With such a word a fool will suffer pangs
   like a woman in labor with a child.
$^{12}$Like an arrow stuck in the flesh of the thigh,
   so is a word inside a fool.
$^{13}$Question a friend, perhaps he did not do it;
   but if he did anything, so that he may do it no more.
$^{14}$Question a neighbor, perhaps he did not say it;
   but if he said it, so that he may not say it again.
$^{15}$Question a friend, for often it is slander;
   so do not believe everything you hear.
$^{16}$A person may make a slip without intending it.
   Who has never sinned with his tongue?
$^{17}$Question your neighbor before you threaten him;
   and let the law of the Most High take its course.

With the usual emphasis Ben Sira returns to "sins of the tongue." 5-9, 10-12, are two strophes condemning in strong terms gossip about others' faults. 10-12 use three lively and humorous images, to drive the lesson home. 13-17, in a series of rhythmic repetitions, protest against rash or harsh judgments. In each case the grievance has arisen solely through hearsay, and dispassionate enquiry may disclose that the report was false or exaggerated, or that the culprit is already repentant. Verse 17a reminds us of the process of admonitions prescribed for the Christian community, Mt 18:15ff. In v. 17b Ben Sira closes the section with an explicit religious appeal. Cf. Lev 19:17.

## TRUE AND FALSE WISDOM
19:20-30

> 20All wisdom is the fear of the Lord,
> and in all wisdom there is the fulfilment of the law.
> 22But the knowledge of wickedness is not wisdom,
> nor is there prudence where sinners take counsel.
> 23There is a cleverness which is abominable,
> but there is a fool who merely lacks wisdom.
> 24Better is the God-fearing man who lacks intelligence,
> than the highly prudent man who transgresses the law.
> 25There is a cleverness which is scrupulous but unjust,
> and there are people who distort
> kindness to gain a verdict.
> 26There is a rascal bowed down in mourning,
> but inwardly he is full of deceit.
> 27He hides his face and pretends not to hear;
> but where no one notices, he will forestall you.
> 28And if by lack of strength he is prevented from sinning,
> he will do evil when he finds an opportunity.
> 29A man is known by his appearance,
> and a sensible man is known by his face,
> when you meet him.
> 30A man's attire and open-mouthed laughter,
> and a man's manner of walking, show what he is.

The identification of wisdom with virtue and of folly with vice was common in the earlier wisdom teaching. But as an over-simplification it was likely to cause misunderstanding, just as it is found puzzling by modern readers. It is perhaps more comprehensible if we invert the terms, and say that a virtuous person is to be considered wise, while a scoundrel or criminal is really a fool. Ben Sira here shows himself aware of the confusion and undertakes to make some necessary distinctions: there *is* a knowledge which is not wise, and a counsel which is not prudent (v. 22). (Similarly the Epistle of James, 3:13-18, distinguishes a wisdom "from above" from a wisdom which is "from below.") In v. 20 he lays down his general principle, then follow the qualifications; vv. 23f. are the most explicit. He neglects however to tell us how "abominable" cleverness can be recognized and distinguished from the approved kind. If challenged, probably he would have responded with some version of "By their fruits you shall know them." In vv. 26ff he considers a single example, that of a wicked man who tries to hide his malice and evil intentions. It is not clear however what connection this figure has with wisdom or folly, which are not mentioned in vv. 26-28. In the last two verses, vv. 29-30, he assures us that external appearance and behavior can (always, or often?) give a clue to a person's wise or foolish character. This idea is followed up in 21:20ff.

## "A TIME TO KEEP SILENCE, A TIME TO SPEAK"
20:1-8

**20**　There is a reproof which is not timely;
　　and there is a man who keeps silent but is wise.
²How much better it is to reprove than to stay angry!
　　And the one who confesses his fault will be kept from
　　　loss.
⁴Like a eunuch's desire to violate a maiden
　　is a man who executes judgments by violence.
⁵There is one who by keeping silent is found wise,
　　while another is detested for being too talkative.
⁶There is one who keeps silent because he has no answer,
　　while another keeps silent because he knows when to
　　　speak.
⁷A wise man will be silent until the right moment,
　　but a braggart and fool goes beyond the right moment.
⁸Whoever uses too many words will be loathed,
　　and whoever usurps the right to speak will be hated.

After the interlude distinguishing true wisdom from its counterfeits, Ben Sira returns to the theme of speech, developing the phrase quoted above from Eccles 3:7. Saying the right thing is not enough, it must be said at the right moment; cf. 1:24. Verses 1-3, 5-8 develop this idea in various ways. Verse 4 is here misplaced; see 30:20.

## PARADOXES
20:9-23

9There may be good fortune for a man in adversity,
  and a windfall may result in a loss.
10There is a gift that profits you nothing,
  and there is a gift that brings a double return.
11There are losses because of glory,
  and there are men who have raised their heads
    from humble circumstances.
12There is a man who buys much for a little,
  but pays for it seven times over.
13The wise man makes himself
    beloved through his words,
  but the courtesies of fools are wasted.
14A fool's gift will profit you nothing,
  for he has many eyes instead of one.
15He gives little and upbraids much,
  he opens his mouth like a herald;
today he lends and tomorrow he asks it back;
  such a one is a hateful man.
16A fool will say, "I have no friend,
  and there is no gratitude for my good deeds;
  those who eat my bread speak unkindly."
17How many will ridicule him, and how often!
18A slip on the pavement is better
    than a slip of the tongue;
  so the downfall of the wicked will occur speedily.
19An ungracious man is like a story
    told at the wrong time,
  which is continually on the lips of the ignorant.

> [20]A proverb from a fool's lips will be rejected,
>     for he does not tell it at its proper time.
> [21]A man may be prevented from sinning by his poverty,
>     so when he rests he feels no remorse.
> [22]A man may lose his life through shame,
>     or lose it because of his foolish look.
> [23]A man may for shame make promises to a friend,
>     and needlessly make him an enemy.

These are a series of miscellaneous observations on human life, often paradoxical and always shrewd. Ben Sira speaks in traditional wisdom style; there is no specific religious tonality here or in the following section. The need for discernment is stressed (vv. 9-12) and the importance of good timing (vv. 19f.); and one type of fool is ridiculed (vv. 14-17).

## RIGHT USE OF LANGUAGE
20:24-31

> [24]A lie is an ugly blot on a man;
>     it is continually on the lips of the ignorant.
> [25]A thief is preferable to a habitual liar,
>     but the lot of both is ruin.
> [26]The disposition of a liar brings disgrace,
>     and his shame is ever with him.
> [27]He who speaks wisely will advance himself,
>     and a sensible man will please great men.
> [28]Whoever cultivates the soil will heap up his harvest,
>     and whoever pleases great men will atone for injustice.
> [29]Presents and gifts blind the eyes of the wise;
>     like a muzzle on the mouth they avert reproofs.
> [30]Hidden wisdom and unseen treasure,
>     what advantage is there in either of them?
> [31]Better is the man who hides his folly
>     than the man who hides his wisdom.

Miscellaneous aphorisms, whose common note still seems to be speech. It is strange that after the outright condemnation of lying (vv. 24-26) Ben Sira seems quite neutral on the topic of flattery and even bribery (vv. 27-29).

28b, "atone for" means "be excused." 29a quotes Deut 16:19.

## EFFECTS OF SIN
21:1-10

> **21** Have you sinned, my son?
>> Do so no more,
>> but pray about your former sins.
> [2]Flee from sin as from a snake;
>> for if you approach sin, it will bite you.
> Its teeth are lion's teeth,
>> and destroy the souls of men.
> [3]All lawlessness is like a two-edged sword;
>> there is no healing for its wound.
> [4]Terror and violence will lay waste riches;
>> thus the house of the proud will be laid waste.
> [5]The prayer of a poor man goes from
>> his lips to the ears of God,
>> and his judgment comes speedily.
> [6]Whoever hates reproof walks in the steps of the sinner,
>> but he that fears the Lord will repent in his heart.
> [7]He who is mighty in speech is known from afar;
>> but the sensible man, when he slips, is aware of it.
> [8]A man who builds his house with other people's money
>> is like one who gathers stones for his burial mound.
> [9]An assembly of the wicked is like tow gathered together,
>> and their end is a flame of fire.
> [10]The way of sinners is smoothly paved with stones,
>> but at its end is the pit of Hades.

For the first time since 18:15 we hear the tone of fatherly admonition, "My son," and in v. 6 the Lord is named for the first time since 19:20. What follows is definitely on the religious level. The section contains three strophes, vv. 1-3, 4-7, 8-10. Ben Sira does not attempt to define sin, but he gives examples — lawlessness, violence, pride, etc. — and piles up images — snake, lion, sword. Note in vv. 4f. the opposition of "proud" and "poor"; the latter is the Lord's friend and his prayer is heard at once. In v. 10, the "way of sinners" may be derived from Prov 7:27, and is perhaps echoed in Mt 7:13. If this verse is original with Ben Sira it seems inconsistent with his doctrine elsewhere (14:16, 17:27f., 22:11, 41:4) which pictures sinners and saints alike descending to the "pit of Hades."

## WISDOM AND FOLLY IN WORD AND DEED
21:11-28

11Whoever keeps the law controls his thoughts,
  and wisdom is the fulfilment of the fear of the Lord.
12He who is not clever cannot be taught,
  but there is a cleverness which increases bitterness.
13The knowledge of a wise man will increase like a flood,
  and his counsel like a flowing spring.
14The mind of a fool is like a broken jar;
  it will hold no knowledge.
15When a man of understanding hears a wise saying,
    he will praise it and add to it;
  when a reveler hears it, he dislikes it and casts it behind
    his back.
16A fool's narration is like a burden on a journey,
  but delight will be found in the speech of the intelligent.
17The utterance of a sensible man
    will be sought in the assembly,
  and they will ponder his words in their minds.
18Like a house that has vanished, so is wisdom to a fool;
  and the knowledge of the ignorant is unexamined talk.
19To a senseless man education is fetters on his feet,
  and like manacles on his right hand.
20A fool raises his voice when he laughs,
  but a clever man smiles quietly
21To a sensible man education is like a golden ornament,
  and like a bracelet on the right arm.
22The foot of a fool rushes into a house,
  but a man of experience stands respectfully before it.
23A boor peers into the house from the door.
  but a cultivated man remains outside.

24It is ill-mannered for a man to listen at a door,
   and a discreet man is grieved by the disgrace.
25The lips of strangers will speak of these things,
   but the words of the prudent
     will be weighed in the balance.
26The mind of fools is in their mouth,
   but the mouth of wise men is in their mind.
27When an ungodly man curses his adversary,
   he curses his own soul.
28A whisperer defiles his own soul
   and is hated in his neighborhood.

The theme here is the contrast of behavior, between wise and foolish. 11-12 are an introduction, in which v. 12 harks back to 19:23. There follows (to v. 21) a series of similes which ingeniously present the contrasts between wise and foolish. 13-14 must owe something to the dramatic image of Jer 2:13: "... they have forsaken me, the fountain of living waters, and hewed out cisterns for themselves, broken cisterns, that can hold no water." In the third strophe, vv. 18-21, the similes go in pairs; read v. 20 after v. 21. "Vanished house ... fetters ... manacles" — such is wisdom to a fool; but to the wise she is "a golden ornament...a bracelet." 22-24 bring some practical judgments on good and bad manners: fools say whatever comes in their heads, the wise think over their words before utterance. 27, the ungodly man is his own worst enemy.

## TYPES OF FOLLY
22:1-18

   **22** The indolent may be compared to a filthy stone,
   and every one hisses at his disgrace.
2The indolent may be compared to the filth of dunghills;
   anyone that picks it up will shake it off his hand.
3It is a disgrace to be the father of an undisciplined son,
   and the birth of a daughter is a loss.
4A sensible daughter obtains her husband,
   but one who acts shamefully brings grief to her father.

⁵An impudent daughter disgraces father and husband,
　　and will be despised by both.
⁶Like music in mourning is a tale told at the wrong time,
　　but chastising and discipline are wisdom at all times.
⁷He who teaches a fool is like
　　　one who glues potsherds together,
　　or who rouses a sleeper from deep slumber.
⁸He who tells a story to a fool tells it to a drowsy man;
　　and at the end he will say, "What is it?"
¹¹Weep for the dead, for he lacks the light;
　　and weep for the fool, for he lacks intelligence;
　weep less bitterly for the dead, for he has attained rest;
　　but the life of the fool is worse than death.
¹²Mourning for the dead lasts seven days,
　　but for a fool or an ungodly man it lasts all his life.
¹³Do not talk much with a foolish man,
　　and do not visit an unintelligent man;
　guard yourself from him to escape trouble,
　　and you will not be soiled when he shakes himself off;
　avoid him and you will find rest,
　　and you will never be wearied by his madness.
¹⁴What is heavier than lead?
　　And what is its name except "Fool"?
¹⁵Sand, salt, and a piece of iron
　　are easier to bear than a stupid man.
¹⁶A wooden beam firmly bonded into a building
　　will not be torn loose by an earthquake;
　so the mind firmly fixed on a reasonable counsel
　　will not be afraid in a crisis.
¹⁷A mind settled on an intelligent thought
　　is like the stucco decoration on the wall of a colonnade.
¹⁸Fences set on a high place
　　will not stand firm against the wind;
　so a timid heart with a fool's purpose
　　will not stand firm against any fear.

The first example here is the "indolent," or sluggard, the able-bodied man who is unwilling to work. He is a particular bugbear of the wisdom writers, who are never tired of denouncing him; see e.g. Prov 24:30-34, 26:13-16. The second example (vv. 3-5) is a daughter who shames her father by bad behavior after she is married. In 4a Ben Sira admits for a moment that a daughter may be "sensible"; but most of the pericope sounds decidedly negative. He enlarges on this theme in 42:9-14. 6b, "chastising and discipline" is probably figurative, cp. 23:2. 7-8 introduce two comic comparisons. 11-12 in hyperbolic terms declare the state of the fool to be worse than that of the dead. 11c, exceptionally, presents the state of the dead as "rest," therefore not wholly negative. Two other wisdom writers had ventured to present the condition of the dead as enviable: Eccles 4:2, and Job 3:11-22. But that was in comparison with sufferings endured by the living; Ben Sira's comparison is with the contemptible behavior of the fool. 12, seven days was the normal period of mourning (Job 2:13, Judith 16:24), but it is curious that in 38:17 Ben Sira himself suggests only one or two days. 12-13 warn against contacts with fools; it is presumed that there is no hope of teaching them wisdom, and would-be teachers will only harm themselves. 14-15 are two proverbial sayings of a standard type; cf. Prov 27:3, and Ahiqar "I have lifted sand and carried salt; but nothing is heavier than grief."

## ON FRIENDSHIP
22:19-26

19A man who pricks an eye will make tears fall,
   and one who pricks the heart makes it show feeling.
20One who throws a stone at birds
    scares them away,
   and one who reviles a friend will
    break off the friendship.
21Even if you have drawn your sword against a friend,
   do not despair, for a renewal of friendship is possible.
22If you have opened your mouth against your friend,
   do not worry, for reconciliation is possible;

but as for reviling, arrogance, disclosure of secrets,
    or a treacherous blow —
  in these cases any friend will flee.
[23]Gain the trust of your neighbor in his poverty,
  that you may rejoice with him in his prosperity;
stand by him in time of affliction,
  that you may share with him in his inheritance.
[24]The vapor and smoke of the furnace precede the fire;
  so insults precede bloodshed.
[25]I will not be ashamed to protect a friend,
  and I will not hide from him;
[26]but if some harm should happen to me because of him,
  whoever hears of it will beware of him.

In 6:5-17 Ben Sira had described how to choose friends
wisely. Now, taking an established friendship for granted,
he warns against destroying it by foolish insults, betrayal or
treachery. 19-20, three similes illustrate the process. 21f.,
friendship may survive violence or anger, but never
treachery. Verse 24 breaks the sequence of thought and may
be out of place.

## TWO PRAYERS
22:27-23:6

[27]O that a guard were set over my mouth,
  and a seal of prudence upon my lips,
that it may keep me from falling,
  so that my tongue may not destroy me!
**23**  O Lord, Father and Ruler of my life,
    do not abandon me to their counsel,
  and let me not fall because of them!
[2]O that whips were set over my thoughts,
  and the discipline of wisdom over my mind!
That they may not spare me in my errors,
  and that it may not pass by my sins;
[3]in order that my mistakes may not be multiplied,
  and my sins may not abound;
then I will not fall before my adversaries,
  and my enemy will not rejoice over me.

4O Lord, Father and God of my life,
    do not give me haughty eyes,
    and remove from me evil desire.
6Let neither gluttony nor lust overcome me,
    and do not surrender me to a shameless soul.

The personal nature of Ben Sira's work is well shown by this insertion of two prayers, individual laments or psalms of petition. The first (22:27-23:1) is a plea to God for help in avoiding sinful speech; the second (23:2-6) asks even more urgently for grace to resist and overcome lustful thoughts. Such material is quite exceptional in wisdom literature, which is concerned with instruction of humankind rather than prayers to God. The book of Proverbs contains only one brief prayer, 30:7-9. What is striking about Ben Sira's compositions is the reverent yet intimate address to God, "Lord, Father and Ruler (God) of my life!" We see that the "our Father" of the Gospels (Mt 6:9) was not such a novelty as is sometimes thought. Cf. the concept of the fatherhood of the Lord in Hos 11:1, Isa 63:16, 64:8, where however the "sons" are Israel as a collectivity. Ben Sira seems to be the first on record to transfer the relationship to a single individual —himself, and to pray to God as "my Father." In 23:1 "their" and "them" refer to mouth, lips and tongue. In these prayers we have the counterpart to the doctrine on human free-will, 15:11-20. Ben Sira saw no contradiction in insisting both on full moral responsibility for human acts, and on the absolute need of divine assistance, to act rightly and avoid sin.


## SINFUL SPEECH
23:7-15

7Listen, my children, to instruction concerning speech;
    the one who observes it will never be caught.
8The sinner is overtaken through his lips,
    the reviler and the arrogant are tripped by them.
9Do not accustom your mouth to oaths,
    and do not habitually utter the name of the Holy One;

[10]for as a servant who is continually examined under
    torture will not lack bruises,
so also the man who always swears and utters the Name
    will not be cleansed from sin.
[11]A man who swears many oaths
        will be filled with iniquity,
    and the scourge will not leave his house;
if he offends, his sin remains on him,
    and if he disregards it, he sins doubly;
if he has sworn needlessly, he will not be justified,
    for his house will be filled with calamities.
[12]There is an utterance which
        is comparable to death;
    may it never be found in the inheritance of Jacob!
For all these errors will be far from the godly,
    and they will not wallow in sins.
[13]Do not accustom your mouth to lewd vulgarity,
    for it involves sinful speech.
[14]Remember your father and mother
    when you sit among great men;
lest you be forgetful in their presence,
    and be deemed a fool on account of your habits;
then you will wish that you had never been born,
    and you will curse the day of your birth.
[15]A man accustomed to use insulting words
    will never become disciplined all his days.

Ben Sira now proceeds to write a brief commentary on
each of the preceding prayers. First, concerning sins of the
tongue: vv. 7-9, we note the emphasis on being "caught" and
"overtaken" by the evil habit, hence the necessity of grace.
Three types of bad language are here censured: first, casual
swearing by the holy Name, YHWH (vv. 9-10) — cf. the
reference to it as the high priest's "glory," 50:20; second,
oaths used merely for emphasis (v. 11); third, obscene or
scurrilous talk (vv. 12-13). The motivation adduced (v. 14) is
surprising: respect for one's parents should prevent one
from using foul language in public. "Cursing the day of
birth" was a violent expression of suffering or grief; cf. Job
3:1ff, Jer 15:10.

## SEXUAL SINS
23:16-27

[16]Two sorts of men multiply sins,
and a third incurs wrath.
The soul heated like a burning fire
will not be quenched until it is consumed;
a man who commits fornication with his near of kin
will never cease until the fire burns him up.
[17]To a fornicator all bread tastes sweet;
he will never cease until he dies.
[18]A man who breaks his marriage vows
says to himself, "Who sees me?
Darkness surrounds me, and the walls hide me,
and no one sees me. Why should I fear?
The Most High will not take notice of my sins."
[19]His fear is confined to the eyes of men,
and he does not realize that the eyes of the Lord
are ten thousand times brighter than the sun;
they look upon all the ways of men,
and perceive even the hidden places.
[20]Before the universe was created, it was known to him;
so it was also after it was finished.
[21]This man will be punished in the streets of the city,
and where he least suspects it, he will be seized.
[22]So it is with a woman who leaves her husband
and provides an heir by a stranger.
[23]For first of all, she has disobeyed the
law of the Most High;
second, she has committed
an offense against her husband;
and third, she has committed adultery through harlotry
and brought forth children by another man.
[24]She herself will be brought before the assembly,
and punishment will fall on her children.
[25]Her children will not take root,
and her branches will not bear fruit.
[26]She will leave her memory for a curse,
and her disgrace will not be blotted out.

$^{27}$Those who survive her will recognize
  that nothing is better than the fear of the Lord,
and nothing sweeter than to heed the commandments of
  the Lord.

The second commentary is on "sins of the flesh," corresponding to 23:2-6. It treats first of men (vv. 16-21), then of women (vv. 22-26). Verse 16 begins with a "numerical proverb"; see below on 25:1-11. The first two types of sinners are defined only vaguely in v. 16ef and v. 17. It is possible ("with his near of kin" is literally "in the body of his flesh") that the first refers to the habitual masturbator. The second type, then, may be the unmarried man given to casual fornication. Verse 17a quotes Prov 9:17. The third type is clearly the adulterer; the description of him skulking about at night is similar to Job 24:15. It is interesting to see that Ben Sira, on this point at least, upholds the equality of the sexes. The older idea of adultery made it equivalent to theft; it was an offense against the wronged husband. A married man did no injury to his own wife by extra-marital adventures. But here Ben Sira makes clear (v. 18a) that husband as well as wife is obliged to exclusive loyalty to the one partner. In vv. 19-20 he insists again on the all-seeing supervision of human lives by God; v. 20 sounds like a summary of Ps 139:4-6. In vv. 22-23 he proceeds to censure the guilty wife, listing different aspects of her offense, and in vv. 24-26 her punishment. Nothing is said of the death penalty, which according to the letter of the law should have been inflicted in such cases. Apparently by the time of Ben Sira this was a dead letter. Verse 27 sums up: "fear of the Lord" and "heeding his commandments" are recurring themes in this book. For Ben Sira they express the devotional and practical sides of religion.

# VI

## PRAISE OF WISDOM
24:1-34

### Wisdom's Speech
24:1-22

**24** Wisdom will praise herself, and will glory
in the midst of her people.
²In the assembly of the Most High
she will open her mouth,
and in the presence of his host she will glory:
³"I came forth from the mouth of the Most High,
and covered the earth like a mist.
⁴I dwelt in high places,
and my throne was in a pillar of cloud.
⁵Alone I have made the circuit of the vault of heaven
and have walked in the depths of the abyss.
⁶In the waves of the sea, in the whole earth,
and in every people and nation
I have gotten a possession.
⁷Among all these I sought a resting place;
I sought in whose territory I might lodge.
⁸Then the Creator of all things
gave me a commandment,
and the one who created me
assigned a place for my tent.

And he said, 'Make your dwelling in Jacob,
    and in Israel receive your inheritance.'
[9]From eternity, in the beginning, he created me,
    and for eternity I shall not cease to exist.
[10]In the holy tabernacle I ministered before him,
    and so I was established in Zion.
[11]In the beloved city likewise he gave me a resting place,
    and in Jerusalem was my dominion.
[12]So I took root in an honored people,
    in the portion of the Lord, who is their inheritance.
[13]I grew tall like a cedar in Lebanon,
    and like a cypress on the heights of Hermon.
[14]I grew tall like a palm tree in Engedi,
    and like rose plants in Jericho;
like a beautiful olive tree in the field,
    and like a plane tree I grew tall.
[15]Like cassia and camel's thorn
        I gave forth the aroma of spices,
    and like choice myrrh I spread a pleasant odor,
like galbanum, onycha, and stacte,
    and like the fragrance of frankincense
        in the tabernacle.
[16] Like a terebinth I spread out my branches,
    and my branches are glorious and graceful.
[17]Like a vine I caused loveliness to bud,
    and my blossoms became glorious and abundant fruit.
[19]Come to me, you who desire me,
    and eat your fill of my produce.
[20]For the remembrance of me is sweeter than honey,
    and my inheritance sweeter than the honeycomb.
[21]Those who eat me will hunger for more,
    and those who drink me will thirst for more.
[22]Whoever obeys me will not be put to shame,
    and those who work with my help will not sin."

This great poem is in some ways the high point of the
book. It continues the series of praises of wisdom (1:1ff,
4:11ff, 6:18ff, 14:20ff), and is linked with similar pieces in
other wisdom books: cf. Job 28, Baruch 3:9-4:4, and espe-

cially Prov 8, which Ben Sira evidently took as his model. He drew also upon Gen 1-2 and a few other sources. The main section, vv. 3-22, belongs to a specific literary form known as the aretalogy, of which we have specimens from Greco-Egyptian literature. It is a hymn of self-praise by a divine being, a goddess, who describes her own beauty, virtues, and readiness to bless and help humanity. Ben Sira has skillfully adapted this form to his concept of divine wisdom which he can personify as a female figure, conveying the Lord's gracious will to humankind. The image is a natural one, since both Hebrew and Greek words for "wisdom" are feminine nouns: *hokmah* and *sophia*.

In Prov 8:2ff Wisdom was speaking to people in an earthly city. But here she is addressing the "host" of the heavenly assembly. Her "glory" takes the form of a narrative (vv. 3-17), followed by the invitation to humankind — but more especially to Israel (vv. 19-22) — to enjoy the riches she offers. The stages in Wisdom's gracious descent are carefully marked. First (vv. 3-4) she is alone with the Creator; then (vv. 5-6) she explores the universe and has contacts with humankind; lastly (vv. 7-8, 10-12) her dwelling is "in Jacob" and her "resting place" in Jerusalem. Verse 9 is certainly out of place; if original it should come between v. 3 and v. 4. Verse 3a refers to the creative words spoken by God in Gen 1; v. 3b, to the "mist" of Gen 2:6. Verse 8 recalls the Sinai covenant, and 10-11 the building of the temple in Jerusalem. 13-17 is not only a poetic list of botanical similes, it contrives to outline the geography of Palestine: from Lebanon and Hermon in the north, to Engedi and Jericho in the south; from the "field" (coastal plain) on the west, to "water" (Jordan) on the east (v. 14d, read ". . . tall beside the water."). The spices and perfumes of v. 15 are the ingredients of the "oil of anointing" (Ex 30:22ff) and the temple incense (Ex 30:34ff). The RSV rightly omits v. 18 (vv. 24f in the Vulgate), a secondary addition which appears in some Greek manuscripts, was translated into Latin and became a popular refrain in the Latin liturgy, honoring Mary the mother of Jesus: "I am the mother of fair love, of fear, of knowledge and of holy hope. In me is all grace of the way

and of the truth; in me is all hope of life and of virtue."
Verses 19-22 contain the invitation; cf. Prov 8:32-36, Isa
55:1-3. It is echoed in Mt 11:28-30, where Jesus speaks as
divine Wisdom: "Come to me, all who labor and are heavy
laden, and I will give you rest. . . ." Verse 21, the expression
is turned around in Jn 4:14, 6:35, yet the meaning is the same
= will not hunger or thirst for other things but will always
desire this wisdom.

Author's Comment
24:23-34

23All this is the book of the covenant of the Most High
        God, the law which Moses commanded us
    as an inheritance for the congregations of Jacob.
25It fills men with wisdom, like the Pishon,
    and like the Tigris at the time of the first fruits.
26It makes them full of understanding,
        like the Euphrates,
    and like the Jordan at harvest time.
27It makes instruction shine forth like light,
    like the Gihon at the time of vintage.
28Just as the first man did not know her perfectly,
    the last one has not fathomed her;
29for her thought is more abundant than the sea,
    and her counsel deeper than the great abyss.
30I went forth like a canal from a river
    and like a water channel into a garden.
31I said, "I will water my orchard
        and drench my garden plot";
    and lo, my canal became a river,
        and my river became a sea.
32I will again make instruction shine forth like the dawn,
    and I will make it shine afar;
33I will again pour out teaching like prophecy,
    and leave it to all future generations.
34Observe that I have not labored for myself alone,
    but for all who seek instruction.

The following section (vv. 23-29) is Ben Sira's comment
on Wisdom's self-praise. His main point is stated imme-

diately in v. 23: this divine Wisdom is in fact the book of the covenant, the Mosaic law. 23bc quotes Deut 33:4. Thus the great treasure of wisdom, so long desired and ardently sought after by Gentile and Israelite alike, turns out to be the revelation long since granted by the Lord to his own people. There is no need to look further. If this seems at first to be a regrettable narrowing down of the traditional universalism of wisdom, we may observe that Ben Sira "expands" the law to fit wisdom, rather than the other way round. He shows no interest in legal minutiae; he never mentions dietary laws or sabbath observance or circumcision or (with one slight exception) legal purity. Fear of the Lord, and justice and charity towards the neighbor: those, for Ben Sira, are the content of this Wisdom/Law.

In vv. 25-27 Ben Sira has another series of images from nature, this time of flooding rivers. He takes the four rivers of Paradise, Gen 2:10-14, and adds to them the Jordan and the Nile (27a, for "shine forth like light" read "overflow like the Nile"). All six in their floodtimes symbolize the abundance and fertility of the torrent of "wisdom ... understanding ... instruction" poured out in this Wisdom/Law. The last strophe, vv. 30-34, continues the water imagery in terms of the irrigation of a garden. Ben Sira is the gardener at first drawing off a trickle of wisdom for his own use, then finding it a flood that required to be shared with others. He believes that his work, "shining like the dawn," will be carried afar and known by future generations — which has certainly come true. The last verse, 34, is repeated in 33:17, but can be in place here too.

## NUMERICAL PROVERBS
25:1-11

**25** My soul takes pleasure in three things,
and they are beautiful in the
sight of the Lord and of men:
agreement between brothers,
friendship between neighbors,
and a wife and husband who live in harmony.

²My soul hates three kinds of men,
  and I am greatly offended at their life:
a beggar who is proud, a rich man who is a liar,
  and an adulterous old man who lacks good sense.
³You have gathered nothing in your youth;
  how then can you find anything in your old age?
⁴What an attractive thing is judgment in gray-haired men,
  and for the aged to possess good counsel!
⁵How attractive is wisdom in the aged,
  and understanding and counsel in honorable men!
⁶Rich experience is the crown of the aged,
  and their boast is the fear of the Lord.
⁷With nine thoughts I have gladdened my heart,
  and a tenth I shall tell with my tongue:
a man rejoicing in his children;
  a man who lives to see the downfall of his foes;
⁸happy is he who lives with an intelligent wife,
  and he who has not made a slip with his tongue,
  and he who has not served a man inferior to himself;
⁹happy is he who has gained good sense,
  and he who speaks to attentive listeners.
¹⁰How great is he who has gained wisdom!
  But there is no one superior to him who fears the Lord.
¹¹The fear of the Lord surpasses everything;
  to whom shall be likened the one who holds it fast?

A numerical proverb was presented in 23:16ff. In Prov 30:7-31 there is a series of seven, and in Job 5:19-26 a particularly fine example in which seven woes are contrasted with seven beatitudes. Here we have a series of three, of which the last is quite elaborate. Verse 1, beautiful in its simplicity, is typical of Ben Sira in his more optimistic moments, and may offset some of his more gloomy reflections on married life. Verse 2 is in every way a contrast: anti-social behavior is opposed to the love of v. 1. Verse 3 is a very pointed reminder to young people; Ben Sira no doubt is thinking of the diligence and perseverance needed for the acquisition of wisdom and virtue. He continues with three aphorisms, and concludes this little section, as so often, with "fear of the Lord." The aphorisms, vv. 4-6, with their generous praise of wise old age, express a cliché of wisdom doctrine. But there were discordant voices too; cf. the disillusionment of that angry young man Elihu, in Job 32:6-9. Verses 7-11 in a series of beatitudes list nine men who deserve to be judged "happy." Unfortunately the fourth one has dropped out of the Greek text, which RSV follows; in v. 8, after "wife," read "who does not plow like a donkey yoked with an ox," i.e. whose married life is harmonious. The image is borrowed from Deut 22:10. The ninth fortunate man is "he who has gained wisdom" — but all nine are surpassed by the tenth, "who fears the Lord." This is Ben Sira's considered judgment, as he stresses in v. 11.

## GOOD AND BAD WOMEN
25:13-26:18

13Any wound, but not a wound of the heart!
    Any wickedness, but not the wickedness of a wife!
14Any attack, but not an attack from those who hate!
    And any vengeance, but not the vengeance of enemies!
15There is no venom worse than a snake's venom,
    and no wrath worse than an enemy's wrath.
16I would rather dwell with a lion and a dragon
    than dwell with an evil wife ...

24From a woman sin had its beginning,
    and because of her we all die.
25Allow no outlet to water,
    and no boldness of speech in an evil wife.
26If she does not go as you direct,
    separate her from yourself.
**26** Happy is the husband of a good wife;
    the number of his days will be doubled.
2A loyal wife rejoices her husband,
    and he will complete his years in peace.
3A good wife is a great blessing;
    she will be granted among the blessings of the
        man who fears the Lord.

⁴Whether rich or poor, his heart is glad,
   and at all times his face is cheerful.
⁵Of three things my heart is afraid,
   and of a fourth I am frightened:
The slander of a city, the gathering of a mob,
   and false accusation — all these are worse than death.
⁶There is grief of heart and sorrow
      when a wife is envious of a rival,
   and a tongue-lashing makes it known to all ...

¹³A wife's charm delights her husband,
   and her skill puts fat on his bones.
¹⁴A silent wife is a gift of the Lord,
   and there is nothing so precious as a disciplined soul.
¹⁵A modest wife adds charm to charm,
   and no balance can weigh the value of a chaste soul.
¹⁶Like the sun rising in the heights of the Lord,
   so is the beauty of a good wife
      in her well-ordered home.
¹⁷Like the shining lamp on the holy lampstand,
   so is a beautiful face on a stately figure.
¹⁸Like pillars of gold on a base of silver,
   so are beautiful feet with a steadfast heart.

Ben Sira here gives us 25 couplets on the wicked woman, and only 10 on her virtuous sister. (However, he has further praise of the latter in 36:21-26.) This is perhaps the most negative part of his work, and the least attractive to the modern reader. Still, we may remember that he is denouncing a failure to love which may be found in either sex, and he certainly does not spare his own, when speaking of vices, cf. 25:2 just above. Verses 13f employ an unusual idiom to express a superlative; lit., "any wound — but not a heart-wound!" With his usual dramatic images ("snake ... dragon ... lion ... bear ... sandy hill"!) Ben Sira continues his diatribe in strophes vv. 16-18, 19-21. Verse 21 is probably warning against choosing a wife for her beauty or wealth, rather than for good character and disposition. Verse 24 is of interest, as the first clear allusion in Scripture to the story of Gen 2-3. Unlike St. Paul (Rom 5:12), Ben Sira blames the woman as the cause of human mortality, which he here seems to consider not as something merely natural but as a punishment for sin. Verse 26 is a clear recommendation to divorce, if the wife will not yield to the husband's wishes. The right to divorce — of the wife by the husband, not vice versa — was taken for granted in Israelite society; the only mention of it in the Law, Deut 24:1-4, aims at restricting it by forbidding remarriage of the same couple. 26:1-4, we are glad to find Ben Sira alternating praise of a good wife with his denunciation of a bad one. He begins with a beatitude, which he expands through four verses; in v. 2, "a loyal wife" is the phrase used in Prov 31:10, which shows the type of woman Ben Sira had in mind. Verse 3 brings in the usual religious reference. Verse 5, the censures resume, with another numerical proverb. The fourth "thing" is the jealous wife, which may imply the man is married to two women. 10-12, the subject seems to change to a "daughter," but the word can mean simply "woman"; the reference may still be to the unfaithful wife. Fortunately, Ben Sira does not stop there but resumes his panegyric of the good wife in vv. 13-18, twice underlining that such a gift is "of the Lord." And he means a high compliment by the comparisons with lampstand and pillars, part of the furniture of the temple.

## ON DISHONESTY
26:28-27:3

> ²⁸At two things my heart is grieved,
>> and because of a third anger comes over me:
> a warrior in want through poverty,
>> and intelligent men who are treated contemptuously;
> a man who turns back from righteousness to sin —
>> the Lord will prepare him for the sword!
> ²⁹A merchant can hardly keep from wrongdoing,
>> and a tradesman will not be declared innocent of sin.
> **27** Many have committed sin for a trifle,
>> and whoever seeks to get rich will avert his eyes.
> ²As a stake is driven firmly into a fissure between stones,
>> so sin is wedged in between selling and buying.

[3]If a man is not steadfast and zealous
in the fear of the Lord,
his house will be quickly overthrown.

Again Ben Sira leads off with a numerical proverb, listing unbecoming changes: wealth to poverty, honor to contempt, justice to sin. To this last he joins a practical example: the man who "goes into business," and finds how difficult it is to remain honest in the world of commerce. 27:2 is a forceful image; v. 3 appeals to fear of the Lord as the only motivation strong enough to resist this temptation.

## ON THE MISUSE OF SPEECH
## 27:4-21

[4]When a sieve is shaken, the refuse remains;
so a man's filth remains in his thoughts.
[5]The kiln tests the potter's vessels;
so the test of a man is in his reasoning.
[6]The fruit discloses the cultivation of a tree;
so the expression of a thought discloses the cultivation
of a man's mind.
[7]Do not praise a man before you hear him reason,
for this is the test of men.
[8]If you pursue justice, you will attain it
and wear it as a glorious robe.
[9]Birds flock with their kind;
so truth returns to those who practice it.
[10]A lion lies in wait for prey;
so does sin for the workers of iniquity.
[11]The talk of the godly man is always wise,
but the fool changes like the moon.
[12]Among stupid people watch for a chance to leave,
but among thoughtful people stay on.
[13]The talk of fools is offensive,
and their laughter is wantonly sinful.
[14]The talk of men given to swearing makes one's hair
stand on end,
and their quarrels make a man stop his ears.
[15]The strife of the proud leads to bloodshed,

and their abuse is grievous to hear.
16Whoever betrays secrets destroys confidence,
and he will never find a congenial friend.
17Love your friend and keep faith with him;
but if you betray his secrets, do not run after him.
18For as a man destroys his enemy,
so you have destroyed the friendship of your neighbor.
19And as you allow a bird to escape from your hand,
so you have let your neighbor go,
and will not catch him again.
20Do not go after him, for he is too far off,
and has escaped like a gazelle from a snare.
21For a wound may be bandaged,
and there is reconciliation after abuse,
but whoever has betrayed secrets is without hope.

Ben Sira begins with a general principle, illustrated by three comparisons, vv. 4-6. The connection of vv. 8-10 with the context is obscure; perhaps they illustrate v. 6b. A constant impulse to good or bad will naturally issue in corresponding acts. Verses 11-15 contrast the talk of God-fearing people with that of "fools ... stupid ... proud." Verses 16-21 treat a very specific case of evil speech: the betrayal of a friend's secrets; cf 22:19-22. With grave eloquence Ben Sira describes the damage that will follow: friendship effectively killed, the victim fled out of sight like a bird or a gazelle.

## ON TREACHERY AND REVENGE
27:22-28:1

22Whoever winks his eye plans evil deeds,
and no one can keep him from them.
23In your presence his mouth is all sweetness,
and he admires your words;
but later he will twist his speech
and with your own words he will give offense.
24I have hated many things, but none
to be compared to him;
even the Lord will hate him.

25Whoever throws a stone straight up
   throws it on his own head;
and a treacherous blow opens up wounds.
26He who digs a pit will fall into it,
   and he who sets a snare will be caught in it.
27If a man does evil, it will roll back upon him,
   and he will not know where it came from.
28Mockery and abuse issue from the proud man,
   but vengeance lies in wait for him like a lion.
29Those who rejoice in the fall of the godly
   will be caught in a snare,
and pain will consume them before their death.
30Anger and wrath, these also are abominations,
   and the sinful man will possess them.
**28** He that takes vengeance will suffer vengeance from
   the Lord,
   and he will firmly establish his sins.

Ben Sira speaks sternly of the malice of a secret enemy who hypocritically pretends to be a friend; cp. the shifty-eyed character in Prov 6:12-15. Verse 24 is a further development of the numerical style: lit., "There are many things I hate, but nothing as much as him; and the Lord hates him too." 25-26 repeat in inverse order two comparisons already used by Ecclesiastes, 10:8f (cf. also Prov 26:27). Both the writers see a kind of built-in mechanism of retribution in created nature, which Ben Sira sums up in vv. 27f. Even in this life the evildoer will be duly and aptly punished. 28:1 shifts the perspective: this "built-in" retribution is of course the Lord's doing and can be considered from a theological point of view.

## ON FORGIVENESS AND PEACE
## 28:2-11

2Forgive your neighbor the wrong he has done,
   and then your sins will be pardoned when you pray.
3Does a man harbor anger against another,
   and yet seek for healing from the Lord?
4Does he have no mercy toward a man like himself,

and yet pray for his own sins?
⁵If he himself, being flesh, maintains wrath,
   who will make expiation for his sins?
⁶Remember the end of your life, and cease from enmity,
   remember destruction and death,
      and be true to the commandments.
⁷Remember the commandments,
   and do not be angry with your neighbor;
   remember the covenant of the Most High,
      and overlook ignorance.
⁸Refrain from strife, and you will lessen sins;
   for a man given to anger will kindle strife,
⁹and a sinful man will disturb friends
   and inject enmity among those who are at peace.
¹⁰In proportion to the fuel for the fire,
      so will be the burning,
   and in proportion to the obstinacy of strife
      will be the burning;
in proportion to the strength of the man will be his anger,
   and in proportion to his wealth
      he will heighten his wrath.
¹¹A hasty quarrel kindles fire,
   and urgent strife sheds blood.

This beautiful passage is one of the most appealing sections in the book, and also the most "Christian" sounding. We see here that the standard of forgiveness proposed by Jesus in the Lord's Prayer, "forgive us the wrong we have done as we forgive those who wrong us" (Mt 6:12), was anticipated two centuries earlier by this teaching of Ben Sira. The argument is dramatized as a confrontation: it begins (v. 2) and ends (vv. 6-7) in direct address to the hearer, which encloses three rhetorical questions (vv. 3-5). These underline the unreasonableness and malice of the sinner who will not forgive others. The same construction is used, to the same effect, in the Matthean parable of the Unmerciful Servant (Mt 18:33): "Should not you have had mercy on your fellow servant . . . . ?", which is like an echo of v. 4. In vv. 6-7 Ben Sira turns to positive recommendations, in eight concise and brisk phrases. The "commandments" in v. 7 are obviously those prescribing love of one's neighbor, for example Lev 19:17f. The parallel mention of the Mosaic covenant is interesting; Ben Sira evidently thinks of it as commanding brotherly and sisterly love of fellow-Jews and being on good terms with one's neighbors. In vv. 8-11 he makes an urgent plea for civic peace, and denounces those who stir up quarrels and strife.

## THE EVIL TONGUE
## 28:12-26

12If you blow on a spark, it will glow;
   if you spit on it, it will be put out;
   and both come out of your mouth.
13Curse the whisperer and deceiver,
   for he has destroyed many who were at peace.
14Slander has shaken many,
   and scattered them from nation to nation,
and destroyed strong cities,
   and overturned the houses of great men.
15Slander has driven away courageous women,
   and deprived them of the fruit of their toil.
16Whoever pays heed to slander will not find rest,
   nor will he settle down in peace.
17The blow of a whip raises a welt,
   but a blow of the tongue crushes the bones.
18Many have fallen by the edge of the sword,
   but not so many as have fallen because of the tongue.
19Happy is the man who is protected from it,
   who has not been exposed to its anger,
      who has not borne its yoke,
   and has not been bound with its fetters;
20for its yoke is a yoke of iron,
   and its fetters are fetters of bronze;
21its death is an evil death,
   and Hades is preferable to it.
22It will not be master over the godly,
   and they will not be burned in its flame.

23Those who forsake the Lord will fall into its power;
     it will burn among them and will not be put out.
It will be sent out against them like a lion;
     like a leopard it will mangle them.
24See that you fence in your property with thorns,
     lock up your silver and gold,
25make balances and scales for your words,
     and make a door and a bolt for your mouth.
26Beware lest you err with your tongue,
     lest you fall before him who lies in wait.

This impressive passage is perhaps the most eloquent of all Ben Sira's many treatments of the subject. It has been imitated and summarized in the NT, in Jas 3:6ff. Verse 13 is a solemn curse on "disturbers of the peace," who with wicked tongues cause endless mischief. The tongue is almost personified in the remaining verses, and described as an evil worse than death itself. Verse 14f., "Slander" is lit. "a third tongue," which became the standard expression in rabbinic writings for a slanderer. The original image no doubt was that of an outsider who intervened maliciously to alienate husband from wife. Iago, villain of Shakespeare's tragedy *Othello*, would be a prime example. Thus the tongue can exile people, destroy cities, dethrone kings, break up marriages; v. 16 refers to the husband who believes the calumnies, and again we may think of Othello. 17-18, 20-21, are extreme statements, which nevertheless contain a lot of truth. In between there is a heartfelt beatitude, v. 19. Verse 22 is a reassurance to "the godly" that they will be preserved from the tongue's ravages, described in v. 23. The final section, vv. 24-26, with appropriate comparisons, urges the hearers to "make a door and a bolt" for their mouths, that they may not be cause of such ravages for others.

## ON LENDING AND GIVING ALMS
29:1-20

**29**   He that shows mercy will lend to his neighbor,
     and he that strengthens him with his hand keeps the
     commandments.

[2]Lend to your neighbor in the time of his need;
  and in turn, repay your neighbor promptly.
[3]Confirm your word and keep faith with him,
  and on every occasion you will find what you need.
[4]Many persons regard a loan as a windfall,
  and cause trouble to those who help them.
[5]A man will kiss another's hands until he gets a loan,
  and will lower his voice in speaking of his
    neighbor's money;
but at the time for repayment he will delay,
  and will pay in words of unconcern,
  and will find fault with the time.
[6]If the lender exerts pressure, he will hardly get back half,
  and will regard that as a windfall.
If he does not, the borrower has robbed him of his money,
  and he has needlessly made him his enemy;
he will repay him with curses and reproaches,
  and instead of glory will repay him with dishonor.
[7]Because of such wickedness, therefore,
    many have refused to lend;
  they have been afraid of being defrauded needlessly.
[8]Nevertheless, be patient with a
    man in humble circumstances,
  and do not make him wait for your alms.
[9]Help a poor man for the commandment's sake,
  and because of his need do not send him away empty.
[10]Lose your silver for the sake of a brother or a friend,
  and do not let it rust under a stone and be lost.
[11]Lay up your treasure according to the commandments
    of the Most High,
  and it will profit you more than gold.
[12]Store up almsgiving in your treasury,
  and it will rescue you from all affliction;
[13]more than a mighty shield and more than a heavy spear,
  it will fight on your behalf against your enemy.
[14]A good man will be surety for his neighbor,
  but a man who has lost his sense of shame will fail him.
[15]Do not forget all the kindness of your surety,
  for he has given his life for you.

16A sinner will overthrow the prosperity of his surety,
17 and one who does not feel grateful
  will abandon his rescuer.
18Being surety has ruined many men
  who were prosperous,
  and has shaken them like a wave of the sea;
it has driven men of power into exile,
  and they have wandered among foreign nations.
19The sinner who has fallen into suretyship
  and pursues gain will fall into lawsuits.
20Assist your neighbor according to your ability,
  but take heed to yourself lest you fall.

In the urban culture of hellenistic cities, including Jerusalem, financial matters were naturally of great importance, and money-lending in particular was a ticklish problem. The Mosaic law insisted that such loans, if made to a fellow-Jew, should be considered part of the virtue of charity (just as much as outright gifts), and no interest should be exacted on them. Ben Sira, curiously, says nothing about interest here; but he shows himself concerned that those with money be generous in lending to the needy, and conversely that the borrowers be conscientious and punctual in repayment. The "commandments" referred to in vv. 1, 9, 11, are such passages as Ex 22:25, Lev 25:35ff., Deut 15:7f. Verses 4-5, 6-7 , 14-17, defend the rights of the generous creditor against the refractory debtor. 8-10, 11-13, renew the recommendation of generosity. Finally, vv. 18-20 end on a note of caution: be generous — but not to the point of ruining yourself. In later Judaism almsgiving to poverty-stricken compatriots was extolled as the greatest act of virtue, and the word *sedaqah*, "righteousness," came to mean specifically "giving of alms."

## ON SELF-SUFFICIENCY AND INDEPENDENCE
29:21-28

21The essentials for life are water and bread
  and clothing and a house to cover one's nakedness.

22Better is the life of a poor man
  under the shelter of his roof
  than sumptuous food in another man's house.
23Be content with little or much.
24It is a miserable life to go from house to house,
  and where you are a stranger you
    may not open your mouth;
25you will play the host and provide
  drink without being thanked,
  and besides this you will hear bitter words:
26"Come here, stranger, prepare the table,
  and if you have anything at hand, let me have it to eat."
27"Give place, stranger, to an honored person;
  my brother has come to stay with me;
    I need my house."
28These things are hard to bear for a man who has feeling:
  scolding about lodging and the reproach of the
  moneylender.

This passage is Ben Sira's reflection on the need for a person to preserve human dignity and self-respect, no matter how limited the means. Anything is preferable to being a dependent, treated with disdain and liable to be expelled from the patron's house when guests are expected. Verse 28 sums up all the foregoing precepts concerning financial affairs.

## ON THE TRAINING OF SONS
30:1-13

**30** He who loves his son will whip him often,
  in order that he may rejoice at the way he turns out.
2He who disciplines his son will profit by him,
  and will boast of him among acquaintances.
3He who teaches his son will make his enemies envious,
  and will glory in him in the presence of friends.
4The father may die, and yet he is not dead,
  for he has left behind him one like himself;
5while alive he saw and rejoiced,
  and when he died he was not grieved;

[6]he has left behind him an avenger against his enemies,
and one to repay the kindness of his friends.
[7]He who spoils his son will bind up his wounds,
and his feelings will be troubled at every cry.
[8]A horse that is untamed turns out to be stubborn,
and a son unrestrained turns out to be wilful.
[9]Pamper a child, and he will frighten you;
play with him, and he will give you grief.
[10]Do not laugh with him, lest you have sorrow with him,
and in the end you will gnash your teeth.
[11]Give him no authority in his youth,
and do not ignore his errors.
[12]Bow down his neck in his youth,
and beat his sides while he is young,
lest he become stubborn and disobey you,
and you have sorrow of soul from him.
[13]Discipline your son and take pains with him,
that you may not be offended by his shamelessness.

This theme was touched on in 7:23 and 22:3; here it is developed. If Ben Sira's directions are taken at face value, they give an impression of great severity and harshness. Certainly he seems to believe in the innate rebelliousness and self-will of children, which only stern discipline can remedy. But in this he is faithful to the sapiential tradition; cf. Prov 13:24, 23:13f., 29:15, 17, and the commentary on Prov 3:11f. in Heb 12:5-11. Verses 4-6 stress the familiar doctrine of immortality through children, ending (v. 6a) with a prevalent pagan idea of the time, which Ben Sira seems to approve. Verse 7 means that a father should not rush to protect his son from every injury or mishap during play or exercise. 8-13 continue in this rather negative approach.

## HEALTH OF MIND AND BODY
## 30:14-25

[14]Better off is a poor man who is well and strong in
constitution
than a rich man who is severely afflicted in body.

[15]Health and soundness are better than all gold,
    and a robust body than countless riches.
[16]There is no wealth better than health of body,
    and there is no gladness above joy of heart.
[17]Death is better than a miserable life,
    and eternal rest than chronic sickness.
[18]Good things poured out upon a mouth that is closed
    are like offerings of food placed upon a grave.
[19]Of what use to an idol is an offering of fruit?
    For it can neither eat nor smell.
So is he who is afflicted by the Lord;
[20]he sees with his eyes and groans,
    like a eunuch who embraces a maiden and groans.
[21]Do not give yourself over to sorrow,
    and do not afflict yourself deliberately.
[22]Gladness of heart is the life of man,
    and the rejoicing of a man is length of days.
[23]Delight your soul and comfort your heart,
    and remove sorrow far from you,
for sorrow has destroyed many,
    and there is no profit in it.
[24]Jealousy and anger shorten life,
    and anxiety brings on old age too soon.
[25]A man of cheerful and good heart
    will give heed to the food he eats.

Ben Sira does not disdain to offer down-to-earth recommendations concerning health and hygiene. His ideas here are reminiscent of Eccles, 4:2, 6:2. Verse 17, cf. the lament in Job 3. The peace of the nether world is preferable to misery on this earth. 18-20 develop the plight of the "afflicted," 14b, 19c. In v. 20b a comparison is repeated from 20:4, which seems more in place here: the eunuch groans, because a simple embrace is all he can do. 23-25, Ben Sira is even aware of the connection between mental tranquillity and good digestion.

## CRITICISM OF RICHES
## 31:1-11

**31** Wakefulness over wealth wastes away one's flesh,
and anxiety about it removes sleep.
²Wakeful anxiety prevents slumber,
and a severe illness carries off sleep.
³The rich man toils as his wealth accumulates,
and when he rests he fills himself with his dainties.
⁴The poor man toils as his livelihood diminishes,
and when he rests he becomes needy.
⁵He who loves gold will not be justified,
and he who pursues money will be led astray by it.
⁶Many have come to ruin because of gold,
and their destruction has met them face to face.
⁷It is a stumbling block to those who are devoted to it,
and every fool will be taken captive by it.
⁸Blessed is the rich man who is found blameless,
and who does not go after gold.
⁹Who is he? And we will call him blessed,
for he has done wonderful things among his people.
¹⁰Who has been tested by it and been found perfect?
Let it be for him a ground for boasting.
Who has had the power to transgress and did not
transgress,
and to do evil and did not do it?
¹¹His prosperity will be established,
and the assembly will relate his acts of charity.

Whatever Ben Sira's own circumstances — he can hardly have been a poor man — and whatever the expectations of his pupils — mostly from wealthy families — he is just as clear and emphatic as any of the prophets on the dangers and temptations of riches. Here he expands on the theme briefly indicated in 30:14f.: there are things in life more precious and valuable than money, yet many people are simply enslaved by it (vv. 5-7). In contrast, he utters a beatitude concerning the wealthy man who has remained unaffected by and detached from his own riches: v. 8, "gold" is *mammon,* the Aramaic word used in Mt 6:24, Lk 16:13. By his emphasis on the rarity of this phenomenon Ben Sira agrees with the Gospel teaching (Mt 19:23) that it is hard for a rich man to enter the kingdom of heaven. V. 11, "assembly," in Hebrew *qahal* and in Greek *ekklesia,* refers to religious and specifically liturgical gatherings. On the walls or floors of synagogues the names of prominent benefactors were often recorded.

## TABLE MANNERS
### 31:12-32:13

[12]Are you seated at the table of a great man?
  Do not be greedy at it,
    and do not say, "There is certainly much upon it!"
[13]Remember that a greedy eye is a bad thing.
  What has been created more greedy than the eye?
  Therefore it sheds tears from every face.
[14]Do not reach out your hand for everything you see,
  and do not crowd your neighbor at the dish.
[15]Judge your neighbor's feelings by your own,
  and in every matter be thoughtful.
[16]Eat like a human being what is set before you,
  and do not chew greedily, lest you be hated.
[17]Be the first to stop eating, for the sake of good manners,
  and do not be insatiable, lest you give offense.
[18]If you are seated among many persons,
  do not reach out your hand before they do.
[19]How ample a little is for a well-disciplined man!
  He does not breathe heavily upon his bed.
[20]Healthy sleep depends on moderate eating;
  he rises early, and feels fit.
The distress of sleeplessness and of nausea
  and colic are with the glutton.
[21]If you are overstuffed with food,
  get up in the middle of the meal,
    and you will have relief.
[22]Listen to me, my son, and do not disregard me,

and in the end you will appreciate my words.
In all your work be industrious,
    and no sickness will overtake you.
23Men will praise the one who is liberal with food,
    and their testimony to his excellence is trustworthy.
24The city will complain of the one
      who is niggardly with food,
    and their testimony to his niggardliness is accurate.
25Do not aim to be valiant over wine,
    for wine has destroyed many.
26Fire and water prove the temper of steel,
    so wine tests hearts in the strife of the proud.
27Wine is like life to men,
    if you drink it in moderation.
What is life to a man who is without wine?
    It has been created to make men glad.
28Wine drunk in season and temperately
    is rejoicing of heart and gladness of soul.
29Wine drunk to excess is bitterness of soul,
    with provocation and stumbling.
30Drunkenness increases the anger of a fool to his injury,
    reducing his strength and adding wounds.
31Do not reprove your neighbor at a banquet of wine,
    and do not despise him in his merrymaking;
speak no word of reproach to him,
    and do not afflict him by making demands of him.
**32** If they make you master of the feast,
    do not exalt yourself;
be among them as one of them;
take good care of them and then be seated;
2   when you have fulfilled your duties, take your place,
that you may be merry on their account
    and receive a wreath for your excellent leadership.
3Speak, you who are older, for it is
    fitting that you should,
but with accurate knowledge,
    and do not interrupt the music.
4Where there is entertainment, do not pour out talk;
    do not display your cleverness out of season.

$^5$A ruby seal in a setting of gold
   is a concert of music at a banquet of wine
$^6$A seal of emerald in a rich setting of gold
   is the melody of music with good wine.
$^7$Speak, young man, if there is need of you,
   but no more than twice, and only if asked.
$^8$Speak concisely, say much in few words;
   be as one who knows and yet holds his tongue.
$^9$Among the great do not act as their equal;
   and when another is speaking, do not babble.
$^{10}$Lightning speeds before the thunder,
   and approval precedes a modest man.
$^{11}$Leave in good time and do not be the last;
   go home quickly and do not linger.
$^{12}$Amuse yourself there, and do what you have in mind,
   but do not sin through proud speech.
$^{13}$And for these things bless him who made you
   and satisfies you with his good gifts.

The subject of wealth has perhaps led on to this treatment of banqueting and the behavior to be observed there, whether as host or guest, with friends or strangers. Despite Ben Sira's conservatism and loyalty to the traditions and ethics of his people, we see that in this respect he takes quite for granted the hellenistic customs of his time and place. Whereas his ancestors, in the heyday of Semitic culture, would have eaten squatting down or else sitting cross-legged on cushions, he and his associates have adopted the Greek custom of lying on couches, propped on their left elbows with their legs stretched out, and using their right hands to help themselves from the tables set in front of them. This was still the custom in NT times, as at Jesus' last supper with his disciples: Jn 13:23-25. Two strophes of six couplets each (31:12-16, 17-21) deal with the subject in general terms; the main stress is on consideration for one's fellow-guests, vv. 15, 17. Moderation is recommended (vv. 19-20); but in case the host's urging has led the guest to eat more than he wished, induced vomiting is recommended, v. 21 (explicitly, in the Hebrew). Verses 23-24 praise a generous host and blame a stingy one. 25-30 deal with the problem of drunkenness, cf. already Prov 23:29-35. As we should expect, Ben Sira favors moderation and discrimination; wine is good in itself, but very liable to abuse. 31 concludes the first subsection with another call to charity.

32:1-2 suppose another hellenistic custom: the election, at the beginning of a banquet, of one of the guests as "master of the feast," a sort of M.C. He would say the grace, propose toasts, prescribe the proportion of water to be mixed with the wine, call on participants for speeches or songs, and in general preside over the festivities. The "steward of the feast" at the wedding of Cana (Jn 2:8-10) was just such a "master." In vv. 3-4 older men are warned against being garrulous; in vv. 7-9, younger ones are told to be reserved. 11-13 sum up, with the usual explicitly religious conclusion.

# VII

## PRUDENT PLANNING
### 32:14-33:6

[14]He who fears the Lord will accept his discipline,
  and those who rise early to seek him will find favor.
[15]He who seeks the law will be filled with it,
  but the hypocrite will stumble at it.
[16]those who fear the Lord will form true judgments,
  and like a light they will kindle righteous deeds.
[17]A sinful man will shun reproof,
  and will find a decision according to his liking.

[18]A man of judgment will not overlook an idea,
  and an insolent and proud man will not cower in fear.
[19]Do nothing without deliberation;
  and when you have acted, do not regret it.
[20]Do not go on a path full of hazards,
  and do not stumble over stony ground.
[21]Do not be overconfident on a smooth way,
[22]  and give good heed to your paths.
[23]Guard yourself in every act,
  for this is the keeping of the commandments.
[24]He who believes the law gives heed
    to the commandments,
  and he who trusts the Lord will not suffer loss.

**33** No evil will befall the man who fears the Lord,
  but in trial he will deliver him again and again.
²A wise man will not hate the law,
  but he who is hypocritical about it
    is like a boat in a storm.
³A man of understanding will trust in the law;
  for him the law is as dependable
  as an inquiry by means of Urim.
⁴Prepare what to say, and thus you will be heard;
  bind together your instruction,
  and make your answer.
⁵The heart of a fool is like a cart wheel,
  and his thoughts like a turning axle.
⁶A stallion is like a mocking friend;
  he neighs under everyone who sits on him.

This section is quite unconnected with the preceding. It returns to the theme of right ordering of life in general, to be assured by fear of the Lord joined with Wisdom/Law. In 32:24-33:3 Ben Sira piles up synonyms for the wise man, "He who believes," etc. He is conscious of course that the Law needs to be interpreted, and judgments on interpretation may differ; but he is convinced that the wise man just described will surely arrive at an understanding which expresses the will of God. V. 3, Urim (and Thummim) were used at an earlier period to give oracular decisions (Num 27:21). But the text here is uncertain; it may refer to Deut 6:8 and the wearing of phylacteries. By emendation it could be read: "The law is dependable like the frontlet on the forehead and the band on the arm." Verses 5 and 6 are two aphorisms which ridicule the wise man's opposites, the foolish and fickle who act without forethought or consistency.

## GOD'S CONTRASTS
33:7-15

⁷Why is any day better than another,
  when all the daylight in the year is from the sun?

[8] By the Lord's decision they were distinguished,
   and he appointed the different seasons and feasts;
[9] some of them he exalted and hallowed,
   and some of them he made ordinary days.
[10] All men are from the ground,
   and Adam was created of the dust.
[11] In the fulness of his knowledge
     the Lord distinguished them
   and appointed their different ways;
[12] some of them he blessed and exalted,
   and some of them he made holy
     and brought near to himself;
but some of them he cursed and brought low,
   and he turned them out of their place.
[13] As clay in the hand of the potter —
   for all his ways are as he pleases —
so men are in the hand of him who made them,
   to give them as he decides.
[14] Good is the opposite of evil,
   and life the opposite of death;
so the sinner is the opposite of the godly.
[15] Look upon all the works of the Most High;
   they likewise are in pairs, one the opposite of the other.

Abruptly Ben Sira returns to the subject discussed in 15:11-20: the problem of divine responsibility for the various evils, physical and moral, that exist in the world. It is easier to account for the physical ones, which he attempts to do here with his doctrine of "opposites," i.e. divinely willed contrasts and oppositions in creation. Verses 7-9 lead off with the differences of days. All are alike in themselves, yet "by the Lord's decision" some are feast days, others ordinary; so with humankind, vv. 10-13, the different treatments experienced by different persons are not (necessarily) connected with merits or demerits. It is simply that the Lord requires variety and contrast in his world. The clay and potter image is a favorite one: cf. Jer 18:1-6, Isa 29:16, Rom 9:20f., etc. In v. 14 it is hinted at least that the just/sinners contrast is another example of the variety and opposition required by God's wisdom.

## CONCLUSION
## 33:16-18

> [16]I was the last on watch;
>    I was like one who gleans after the grape-gathers;
> by the blessing of the Lord I excelled,
>    and like a grape-gatherer I filled my wine press.
> [17]Consider that I have not labored for myself alone,
>    but for all who seek instruction.
> [18]Hear me, you who are great among the people,
>    and you leaders of the congregation, hearken.

If this little section is in its right place it suggests that at one time the book ended here, and that the 18 chapters which now follow represent a later enlargement, a sort of second edition of the work. The present conclusion, in 50:27-29, is phrased quite differently. 16, the image of the gleaner gathering grapes overlooked by the regular vintagers is a pleasing one; Ben Sira modestly attributes his abundant harvest to the Lord's blessing. Verse 17 repeats 24:34, and v. 18 (if in place here) invites the "authorities" to pay attention to his work.

# VIII

## ON PRESERVING ONE'S INDEPENDENCE
## 33:19-23

> $^{19}$To son or wife, to brother or friend,
>     do not give power over yourself,
>         as long as you live;
> and do not give your property to another,
>     lest you change your mind and must ask for it.
> $^{20}$While you are still alive and have breath in you,
>     do not let any one take your place.
> $^{21}$For it is better that your children should ask from you
>     than that you should look to the hand of your sons.
> $^{22}$Excel in all that you do;
>     bring no stain upon your honor.
> $^{23}$At the time when you end the days of your life,
>     in the hour of death, distribute your inheritance.

In six concise couplets Ben Sira admonishes against allowing control of one's affairs to slip out of one's own hands. The situation envisaged is that of an old man who might too trustingly confide administration of his goods or fortune to younger hands — only to regret the same bitterly, when too late. A classical example would be the story of King Lear.

# ON THE TREATMENT OF SLAVES
## 33:24-31

[24]Fodder and a stick and burdens for an ass;
    bread and discipline and work for a servant.
[25]Set your slave to work, and you will find rest;
    leave his hands idle, and he will seek liberty.
[26]Yoke and thong will bow the neck,
    and for a wicked servant there are racks and tortures.
[27]Put him to work, that he may not be idle,
    for idleness teaches much evil.
[28]Set him to work, as is fitting for him,
    and if he does not obey, make his fetters heavy.
[29]Do not act immoderately toward anybody,
    and do nothing without discretion.
[30]If you have a servant, let him be as yourself,
    because you have bought him with blood.
[31]If you have a servant, treat him as a brother,
    for as your own soul you will need him.
If you ill-treat him, and he leaves and runs away,
    which way will you go to seek him?

Ben Sira here returns to a theme he touched on in 7:20f. The slave in the ancient world had no "rights," he was someone's property just like an ox or an ass — though always there was a theoretical possibility of manumission. The Mosaic law in several passages attempted to ease the slave's lot and defend him or her against ill-treatment. Ben Sira believes in keeping a slave hard at work, so as to leave him no time for mischief or seeking liberty. At the same time, he suggests reasons (vv. 29-31) for humane treatment. Like the NT writers (Eph 6:5-9, Col 3:22—4:1; Phlm 16) Ben Sira did not seek revolutionary change in social structures, such as abolition of slavery would have involved. But by providing norms of charity and respect for human dignity he aimed at improving the slaves' situation.

## ON USELESS DREAMS
34:1-8

**34** A man of no understanding has vain and false hopes,
and dreams give wings to fools.

²As one who catches at a shadow and pursues the wind,
so is he who gives heed to dreams.

³The vision of dreams is this against that,
the likeness of a face confronting a face.

⁴From an unclean thing what will be made clean?
And from something false what will be true?

⁵Divinations and omens and dreams are folly,
and like a woman in travail the mind has fancies.

⁶Unless they are sent from the Most High as a visitation,
do not give your mind to them.

⁷For dreams have deceived many,
and those who put their hope in them have failed.

⁸Without such deceptions the law will be fulfilled,
and wisdom is made perfect in truthful lips.

In many societies dreams have been regarded as precious communications of hidden knowledge, deserving of close attention. The Biblical narratives themselves sometimes present dreams as means of divine revelation. In Genesis alone we have Jacob's dream at Bethel (Gen 28:12), Joseph's dreams (ib. 37:5-10), Pharaoh's servants' dreams (ib. 40:5-19) and his own (ib. 41:1-7). Even in NT divine instructions are presented as being given (to Joseph and to the Magi) in the form of dreams; see Mt 1:20-24, 2:12f, 19-12. Ben Sira has to make allowance for the Genesis stories, which he does in passing (v. 6a); otherwise he is entirely hostile to oneiromancy. We see why, in v. 8: the written Law and spoken Wisdom are the authentic channels for detecting the will of God, and dreams can only detract from those authorities. Ecclesiastes (5:2) had already scoffed at dreams as the product of daytime worries, and Ben Sira seems to agree in v. 5.

## SECURITY OF THE FAITHFUL
## 34:9-17

9An educated man knows many things,
   and one with much experience
      will speak with understanding.
10He that is inexperienced knows few things,
   but he that has traveled acquires much cleverness.
11I have seen many things in my travels,
   and I understand more than I can express.
12I have often been in danger of death,
   but have escaped because of these experiences.
13The spirit of those who fear the Lord will live,
   for their hope is in him who saves them.
14He who fears the Lord will not be timid,
   nor play the coward, for he is his hope.
15Blessed is the soul of the man who fears the Lord!
   To whom does he look? And who is his support?
16The eyes of the Lord are upon those who love him,
   a mighty protection and strong support,
a shelter from the hot wind and a shade from noonday
   sun,
   a guard against stumbling and a defense against falling.
17He lifts up the soul and gives light to the eyes;
   he grants healing, life, and blessing.

The mention of perfect wisdom leads on to this meditation on salvation and security in this life. Again Ben Sira offers an interesting combination of merely human elements — experience in foreign travel — with divine grace, namely, protection freely granted to "those who love him." 11-12 is a tantalizing fragment of autobiography (see also 39:4). Where did Ben Sira's travels take him? and what dangers did he run? In vv. 13-17, coming to speak of the care of the Lord for his faithful, Ben Sira quotes liberally from the Psalms; e.g., v. 14, cf. Ps 23:4, 112:7f.; v. 16, cf. Ps 33:18, 34:15, 121:5f.

# WORSHIP IN SPIRIT AND IN TRUTH
34:18-35:20

$^{18}$If one sacrifices from what has
     been wrongfully obtained, the offering is blemished;
   the gifts of the lawless are not acceptable.
$^{19}$The Most High is not pleased
     with the offerings of the ungodly;
   and he is not propitiated for sins by a multitude of
     sacrifices.
$^{20}$Like one who kills a son before his father's eyes
   is the man who offers a sacrifice
     from the property of the poor.
$^{21}$The bread of the needy is the life of the poor;
     whoever deprives them of it is a man of blood.
$^{22}$To take away a neighbor's living is to murder him;
     to deprive an employee of his wages is to shed blood.
$^{23}$When one builds and another tears down,
     what do they gain but toil?
$^{24}$When one prays and another curses,
     to whose voice will the Lord listen?
$^{25}$If a man washes after touching a dead body,
     and touches it again,
   what has he gained by his washing?
$^{26}$So if a man fasts for his sins,
     and goes again and does the same things,
who will listen to his prayer?
     And what has he gained by humbling himself?

**35** He who keeps the law makes many offerings;
   he who heeds the commandments
     sacrifices a peace offering.
$^{3}$To keep from wickedness is pleasing to the Lord,
     and to forsake unrighteousness is atonement.
$^{4}$Do not appear before the Lord empty-handed,
$^{5}$  for all these things are to be done
     because of the commandment.
$^{6}$The offering of a righteous man anoints the altar,
     and its pleasing odor rises before the Most High.

7The sacrifice of a righteous man is acceptable,
  and the memory of it will not be forgotten.
8Glorify the Lord generously,
  and do not stint the first fruits of your hands.
9With every gift show a cheerful face,
  and dedicate your tithe with gladness.
10Give to the Most High as he has given,
  and as generously as your hand has found.
11For the Lord is the one who repays,
  and he will repay you sevenfold.
12Do not offer him a bribe, for he will not accept it;
  and do not trust to an unrighteous sacrifice;
for the Lord is the judge,
  and with him is no partiality.
13He will not show partiality in the case of a poor man;
  and he will listen to the prayer of one who is wronged.
14He will not ignore the supplication of the fatherless,
  nor the widow when she pours out her story.
15Do not the tears of the widow run down her cheek
  as she cries out against him
    who has caused them to fall?
16He whose service is pleasing to the Lord will be
  accepted,
  and his prayer will reach to the clouds.
17The prayer of the humble pierces the clouds,
  and he will not be consoled until it reaches the Lord;
he will not desist until the Most High visits him,
  and does justice for the righteous,
    and executes judgment.
18And the Lord will not delay,
  neither will he be patient with them,
till he crushes the loins of the unmerciful
  and repays vengeance on the nations;
till he takes away the multitude of the insolent,
  and breaks the scepters of the unrighteous;
19till he repays man according to his deeds,
  and the works of men according to their devices;
till he judges the case of his people
  and makes them rejoice in his mercy.

[20]Mercy is as welcome when he afflicts them
as clouds of rain in the time of drought.

All the great religions of humankind combine in varying degrees the practice of external cult, in which worship, praise and petition are directed to the deity, with rules of societal conduct aimed at achieving justice and fair dealing with fellow-humans. As cult is normally the easier of these two functions, while morality usually makes inconvenient demands for self-denial, there is a constant tendency to substitute the former for the latter. According to the testimony of Israel's prophets and historians this tendency sometimes prevailed to an alarming degree in the public life of Judah and Israel, especially in the pre-exilic period. We need only refer to passages such as Isa 1, Hosea 4, Jer 2 and 7, etc. Now, in this eloquent passage treating of the problem of insincere and hypocritical worship, Ben Sira aligns himself firmly with those great prophets. Already Prov 15:8 had laid down the principle, "The sacrifice of the wicked is an abomination to the Lord,/ but the prayer of the upright is his delight." Ben Sira develops that doctrine, in 34 couplets, with clarity and emphasis. In 34:19 it is clear that the ungodly offer sacrifices without repentance or conversion; hence, there is no forgiveness. In vv. 20-22 we have a slashing denunciation of the rich man who cheats his employees, then out of his unholy profits offers sacrifices. Ben Sira, three times, bluntly calls him a murderer. In vv. 23-26 contradictory actions are listed; the result is that things remain as before, and the sinner is not purified from sin. Real repentance requires a radical change of heart.

In 35:1-15 Ben Sira dwells on the positive aspect of morality and social justice as the necessary foundation and presupposition for acceptable sacrificial worship. First the law, the commandments, kindness, alms, avoiding wickedness and unrighteousness are the equivalent of the various liturgical offerings. The latter aptly symbolize those works of charity but they cannot substitute for them. In vv. 4-7 the just man's offerings are praised — because backed by his just deeds. In vv. 8-10 Ben Sira expresses his own joy in the temple liturgy; he is happy because in it he gives outward expression to his gratitude for God's gifts. 11-12 again warn against the "bribery" concept of sacrifice, which is nothing but an insult to the Lord. 13-15 return to the idea of oppression of the weak, as in 34:20-22; 16-17 are a strong affirmation of God's concern for them. 18, 19-20, repeat condemnation of the "unmerciful...insolent...unrighteous," and end with assurance of divine mercy for "his people."

# IX

## A COLLECTIVE PETITION
36:1-17

**36** Have mercy upon us, O Lord, the God of all, and
look upon us,
2 and cause the fear of thee to fall upon all the nations.
3Lift up thy hand against foreign nations
and let them see thy might.
4As in us thou hast been sanctified before them,
so in them be thou magnified before us;
5and let them know thee, as we have known
that there is no God but thee, O Lord.
6Show signs anew and work further wonders;
make thy hand and thy right arm glorious.
7Rouse thy anger and pour out thy wrath;
destroy the adversary and wipe out the enemy.
8Hasten the day, and remember the appointed time,
and let people recount thy mighty deeds.
9Let him who survives be consumed in the fiery wrath,
and may those who harm thy people meet destruction.
10Crush the heads of the rulers of the enemy,
who say, "There is no one but ourselves."
11Gather all the tribes of Jacob,
and give them their inheritance, as at the beginning.

¹²Have mercy, O Lord, upon the people called by thy
    name, upon Israel,
  whom thou hast likened to a first-born son.
¹³Have pity on the city of thy sanctuary,
  Jerusalem, the place of thy rest.
¹⁴Fill Zion with the celebration of thy wondrous deeds,
  and thy temple with thy glory.
¹⁵Bear witness to those whom thou didst create in the
    beginning,
  and fulfil the prophecies spoken in thy name.
¹⁶Reward those who wait for thee,
  and let thy prophets be found trustworthy.
¹⁷Hearken, O Lord, to the prayer of thy servants,
  according to the blessing of Aaron for thy people,
and all who are on the earth will know
  that thou art the Lord, the God of the ages.

This psalm of lament or petition is the only section of the
book which looks forward to a dramatic divine intervention
on behalf of Israel: what is usually called the Messianic
hope. But whether it is Ben Sira's own composition remains
uncertain. The first word of v. 1 is *hoshi'enu,* i.e. Hosanna,
as in Ps 118:25. The reference in v. 4 is no doubt to the
Babylonian exile; by thus punishing his people's infidelity
the Lord had "sanctified" himself, i.e. demonstrated his
intolerance of sin. Now, if he will only punish the Gentile
oppressors, that in turn will "magnify" him before his people. 6-10 appeal for this intervention in the terms traditionally used of the Exodus from Egypt: "signs . . . wonders . . .
right hand . . . anger," etc. Presumably Ben Sira has in mind
the Seleucid rulers to whom the Jews were subject in his day,
though so far as we know the latter were not harshly treated
under Antiochus III (died 187 B.C.), and enjoyed the privilege of governing themselves according to Mosaic law. But
no doubt the paying of taxes and tribute to a Gentile power
was felt as oppression. 11-14 have a decidedly nostalgic
tone; the "tribes of Jacob" would include the population of
the northern kingdom, dispersed and absorbed in the Assyrian empire five centuries earlier. 12, the name Israel was

interpreted as "who fights with El," cf. Gen 32:28. The last strophe, vv. 15-17, lists motives why the Lord should hearken to this prayer.

This passage had a marked influence on one of the most popular prayers of Judaism, the *shemoneh 'esreh* or "Eighteen (Blessings)" recited by the Orthodox three times daily.

## CHOICE OF A WIFE
## 36:18-26

[18]The stomach will take any food,
  yet one food is better than another.
[19]As the palate tastes the kinds of game,
  so an intelligent mind detects false words.
[20]A perverse mind will cause grief,
  but a man of experience will pay him back.
[21]A woman will accept any man,
  but one daughter is better than another.
[22]A woman's beauty gladdens the countenance,
  and surpasses every human desire.
[23]If kindness and humility mark her speech,
  her husband is not like other men.
[24]He who acquires a wife gets his best possession,
  a helper fit for him and a pillar of support.
[25]Where there is no fence, the property will be plundered;
  and where there is no wife, a man will wander about
    and sigh.
[26]For who will trust a nimble robber
  that skips from city to city?
So who will trust a man that has no home,
  and lodges wherever night finds him?

A short section, in which Ben Sira discusses the benefits of a good marriage. 18-20 is a little introduction stressing the importance of discernment in entering on any relationship, *a fortiori* those of marriage, friendship and counseling, which are to be discussed in turn. 22-23 praise the gifts of beauty and gracious speech; it is surprising that Ben Sira stops at these qualities and does not go on to mention "fear of the Lord." In Prov 31:30 the last-named is ranked ahead of charm and beauty. 24-26, Ben Sira describes the advantages of a good wife and the sad plight of a man without one, using some picturesque images to depict the latter. Verse 25, "wander about and sigh" is in the Hebrew a quotation from Gen 4:14, there applied to Cain.

## TRUE AND FALSE FRIENDS
37:1-6

**37** Every friend will say, "I too am a friend";
   but some friends are friends only in name.
[2]Is it not a grief to the death when a companion
   and friend turns to enmity?
[3]O evil imagination, why were you formed
   to cover the land with deceit?
[4]Some companions rejoice in the happiness of a friend,
   but in time of trouble are against him.
[5]Some companions help a friend
   for their stomachs' sake,
   and in the face of battle take up the shield.
[6]Do not forget a friend in your heart,
   and be not unmindful of him in your wealth.

The theme was already treated in chaps. 6, 9, 11 and 22. This time Ben Sira is concerned with the case of a treacherous friend. Verse 3, "imagination" is the *yeser,* "inclination," of 15:14, which impels to deceit.

## CHOICE OF COUNSELORS
37:7-15

[7]Every counselor praises counsel,
   but some give counsel in their own interest.
[8]Be wary of a counselor,
   and learn first what is his interest —
   for he will take thought for himself —
lest he cast the lot against you
[9]   and tell you, "Your way is good,"
   and then stand aloof to see what will happen to you.

10Do not consult with one who looks
    at you suspiciously;
  hide your counsel from those
    who are jealous of you.
11Do not consult with a woman about her rival
  or with a coward about war,
with a merchant about barter
  or with a buyer about selling,
with a grudging man about gratitude
  or with a merciless man about kindness,
with an idler about any work
  or with a man hired for a year
    about completing his work,
with a lazy servant about a big task —
  pay no attention to these in
    any matter of counsel.
12But stay constantly with a godly man
  whom you know to be a keeper of the commandments,
whose soul is in accord with your soul,
  and who will sorrow with you if you fail.
13And establish the counsel of your own heart,
  for no one is more faithful to you than it is.
14For a man's soul sometimes keeps him better informed
  than seven watchmen sitting high on a watchtower.
15And besides all this pray to the Most High
  that he may direct your way in truth.


Ben Sira warns first against a would-be counselor who proffers advice unasked (vv. 7-9), then against enemies and the envious (v. 10). Next, with typical realism, he lists nine types of persons who should not be consulted on nine specific topics. As is plain, they will not give helpful or disinterested advice. But as sources of good counsel, he lists three, in ascending order: a Godfearing and conscientious friend; one's own conscience and insight (with a delightful comparison); finally, God's guidance, to be given in answer to prayer.

## PRACTICAL WISDOM
### 37:16-26

$^{16}$Reason is the beginning of every work,
 and counsel precedes every undertaking.
$^{17}$As a clue to changes of heart
$^{18}$ four turns of fortune appear,
good and evil, life and death;
 and it is the tongue that continually rules them.
$^{19}$A man may be shrewd and the teacher of many,
 and yet be unprofitable to himself.
$^{20}$A man skilled in words may be hated;
 he will be destitute of all food,
$^{21}$for grace was not given him by the Lord,
 since he is lacking in all wisdom.
$^{22}$A man may be wise to his own advantage,
 and the fruits of his understanding
 may be trustworthy on his lips.
$^{23}$A wise man will have praise heaped upon him,
 and all who see him will call him happy.
$^{25}$The life of a man is numbered by days,
 but the days of Israel are without number.
$^{26}$He who is wise among his people
 will inherit confidence,
 and his name will live for ever.

In this section wisdom is not personified, it is considered merely as a gift or quality in certain people. In the brief introduction, vv. 16-18, Ben Sira cites examples of his "opposites" (cf. 33:14f); which will prevail at a given moment depends on what a man chooses to say. He then compares three types of sages: vv. 19-21, the ineffective; v. 22, the "wise to his own advantage"; vv. 23-26, the wise for "his own people." To this last, Ben Sira promises immortal fame.

## TEMPERANCE AND TREATMENT OF ILLNESS
### 37:27-38:15

$^{27}$My son, test your soul while you live;
 see what is bad for it and do not give it that.

$^{28}$For not everything is good for everyone,
and not every person enjoys everything.
$^{29}$Do not have an insatiable appetite for any luxury,
and do not give yourself up to food;
$^{30}$For overeating brings sickness,
and gluttony leads to nausea.
$^{31}$Many have died of gluttony,
but he who is careful to avoid it
prolongs his life.

**38** Honor the physician with the honor due him,
according to your need of him,
for the Lord created him;
$^2$for healing comes from the Most High,
and he will receive a gift from the king.
$^3$The skill of the physician lifts up his head,
and in the presence of great men he is admired.
$^4$The Lord created medicines from the earth,
and a sensible man will not despise them.
$^5$Was not water made sweet with a tree
in order that his power might be known?
$^6$And he gave skill to men
that he might be glorified in his marvelous works.
$^7$By them he heals and takes away pain;
$^8$   the pharmacist makes of them a compound.
His works will never be finished;
and from him health is upon the face of the earth.
$^9$My son, when you are sick do not be negligent,
but pray to the Lord, and he will heal you.
$^{10}$Give up your faults and direct your hands aright,
and cleanse your heart from all sin.
$^{11}$Offer a sweet-smelling sacrifice,
and a memorial portion of fine flour,
and pour oil on your offering,
as much as you can afford.
$^{12}$And give the physician his place,
for the Lord created him;
let him not leave you, for there is need of him.
$^{13}$There is a time when success lies in the
hands of the physicians,

[14] for they too will pray to the Lord
that he should grant them success in diagnosis
and in healing, for the sake of preserving life.
[15]He who sins before his Maker,
may he fall into the care of a physician.

For the first time since 31:22 Ben Sira addresses "My son"; cp. below, 38:9, 16. In plain and reasonable terms he composes a short treatise on temperance, encouraging each one to discover what regime is most conducive to his health and long life. This leads on to the consideration of medicine and illness, 38:1-15. As always, our author is concerned to reconcile the traditional faith in divine causality with the more mundane attitude of reliance on human means. In the case of illness he insists that the summoning of a medical man and the use of the remedies he prescribes in no way indicate impiety or lack of faith in God's power to heal. On the contrary, healing herbs, drugs and the skill of the physician may be just the means by which the Lord if he so chooses will grant healing and recovery. Obviously, there were people who disagreed, on religious grounds, with this judgment; cf. perhaps 2 Chr 16:12. Ben Sira has such a high opinion of the medical profession as to put it on a level with his own avocation of scribe; cp. 38:1-3 with 39:4. In 4-8 he appeals to the fact that the Creator has implanted specific healing qualities in various plants: how can it be impious to make use of them? He cites (v. 5) the incident recorded in Ex 15:25, obviously not regarding it as anything miraculous but as the effect of a purifying quality inherent in the wood. At the same time, to ensure these effects (which are not automatic) God should be invoked in prayer, even by physicians themselves (v. 14).

## ON MOURNING FOR THE DEAD

38:16-23

[16]My son, let your tears fall for the dead,
and as one who is suffering
grievously begin the lament.

Lay out his body with the honor due him,
  and do not neglect his burial.
[17]Let your weeping be bitter and your wailing fervent;
  observe the mourning according to his merit,
for one day or two, to avoid criticism;
  then be comforted for your sorrow.
[18]For sorrow results in death,
  and sorrow of heart saps one's strength.
[19]In calamity sorrow continues,
  and the life of the poor man weighs down his heart.
[20]Do not give your heart to sorrow;
  drive it away, remembering the end of life.
[21]Do not forget, there is no coming back;
  you do the dead no good, and you injure yourself.
[22]"Remember my doom, for yours is like it:
  yesterday it was mine, and today it is yours."
[23]When the dead is at rest, let his remembrance cease,
  and be comforted for him when his spirit has departed.

Ben Sira now turns to the subject of burial customs and mourning. Practical as ever, he warns against excessive or prolonged grief, which cannot benefit the dead and may harm the living. 20-21 seem rather hard, in view of the importance he elsewhere attaches to "immortality" in the memory of posterity. But in this context he is deprecating prolonged lamentation, not simple admiration of the deceased's qualities and achievements. Verse 22, the chief lesson to be taken from death is reflection on the inevitability of one's own.


## FOUR TYPES OF CRAFTSMEN
38:24-34

[24]The wisdom of the scribe depends on
  the opportunity of leisure:
  and he who has little business may become wise.
[25]How can he become wise who handles the plow,
  and who glories in the shaft of a goad,

who drives oxen and is occupied with their work,
and whose talk is about bulls?
26He sets his heart on plowing furrows,
and is careful about fodder for the heifers.
27So too is every craftsman and master workman
who labors by night as well as by day;
those who cut the signets of seals,
each is diligent in making a great variety;
he sets his heart on painting a lifelike image,
and he is careful to finish his work.
28So too is the smith sitting by the anvil,
intent upon his handiwork in iron;
the breath of the fire melts his flesh,
and he wastes away in the heat of the furnace;
he inclines his ear to the sound of the hammer,
and his eyes are on the pattern of the object.
He sets his heart on finishing his handiwork,
and he is careful to complete its decoration.
29So too is the potter sitting at his work
and turning the wheel with his feet;
he is always deeply concerned over his work,
and all his output is by number.
30He moulds the clay with his arm
and makes it pliable with his feet;
he sets his heart to finish the glazing,
and he is careful to clean the furnace.
31All these rely upon their hands,
and each is skilful in his own work.
32Without them a city cannot be established,
and men can neither sojourn nor live there.
33Yet they are not sought out for the council of the people,
nor do they attain eminence in the public assembly.
They do not sit in the judge's seat,
nor do they understand the sentence of judgment;
they cannot expound discipline or judgment,
and they are not found using proverbs.
34But they keep stable the fabric of the world,
and their prayer is in the practice of their trade.

In ancient Egyptian literature there was a type of satirical writing called the Satire on the Trades. This contained elaborate ridicule of all manual labor, such as that of the smith, the potter, the fisherman, etc., and glorification of the superior profession of the scribe and bureaucrat. It was intended as propaganda and encouragement for the youngsters laboring to acquire the difficult art of writing Egyptian hieroglyphics. They were assured that this skill was enviable and productive of social promotion and success. Ben Sira here has a similar treatment of four professions — ploughman, sealcutter, blacksmith and potter — which he compares with the far more admirable calling of the scribe who studies the Law. But in one point he differs notably from the Egyptian material: with his usual moderation and kindness he does not ridicule or sneer at manual labor. He goes out of his way to praise it and to underline its importance in civilized society (vv. 32, 34). Only, the scribe's occupation is still more important and admirable. After the introductory v. 24 there are four strophes on the four crafts (vv. 25-30) and a fifth one (vv. 31-34) to sum up. Note the refrains "sets his heart...is careful..." at the ends of 26, 27, 28, 30. The fifth strophe stresses the utility and indeed necessity of their labor. 31b is lit. "each one is *wise* at his own task." Ben Sira deliberately uses the word, showing the wide gamut of wisdom from the Creator himself to the humblest laborers. With the latter however it has narrow limits. It does not qualify them to be judges or statesmen or rulers. These nobler and higher occupations are open only to members of the leisured class who have no need to work for a living, but have time and energy to study, reflect and discuss, and so acquire a higher wisdom. At the end of v. 33 the Greek translator made a comical mistake (followed by RSV), misreading *moshelim*, "rulers," as *meshalim*, "proverbs." Read "... not found among the rulers."

## THE WISE AND LEARNED SCRIBE
39:1-11

> **39**   On the other hand he who devotes himself
>      to the study of the law of the Most High

will seek out the wisdom of all the ancients,
    and will be concerned with prophecies;
2he will preserve the discourse of notable men
    and penetrate the subtleties of parables;
3he will seek out the hidden meanings of proverbs
    and be at home with the obscurities of parables.
4He will serve among great men
    and appear before rulers;
he will travel through the lands of foreign nations,
    for he tests the good and the evil among men.
5He will set his heart to rise early
    to seek the Lord who made him.
    and will make supplication before the Most High;
he will open his mouth in prayer
    and make supplication for his sins.
6If the great Lord is willing,
    he will be filled with the spirit of understanding;
he will pour forth words of wisdom
    and give thanks to the Lord in prayer.
7He will direct his counsel and knowledge aright,
    and meditate on his secrets.
8He will reveal instruction in his teaching,
    and will glory in the law of the Lord's covenant.
9Many will praise his understanding,
    and it will never be blotted out;
his memory will not disappear,
    and his name will live through all generations.
10Nations will declare his wisdom,
    and the congregation will proclaim his praise;
11if he lives long, he will leave a
        name greater than a thousand,
    and if he goes to rest, it is enough for him.

In contrast to the laborers and artisans of the preceding passage, who need to earn their bread by the sweat of their brows, Ben Sira now describes the ideal scribe. Free from the necessity of manual toil, he has leisure, diligence and inclination, by study, travel and prayer, to become learned and wise. This eloquent eulogy is structured in four strophes, on the scribe's studies, travels, writings and fame, respectively. In v. 1, as in the grandson's Prologue, we have the threefold division of the Hebrew biblical canon, only this time in the sequence Law, Wisdom, Prophecies. Verses 2-3 concentrate on the Wisdom literature. The first strophe, vv. 1-3, focuses on the most important factor in the sage's training, study of the word of God. In the second strophe, vv. 4-5, we have a "natural" factor, foreign travel, plus another religious one, prayer. Note how simply Ben Sira can refer to human sins, and the universal need for forgiveness and reconciliation. For him, wisdom unaccompanied by fear of the Lord is simply unthinkable; other factors would be in vain unless (v. 6a) the Lord is pleased to infuse wisdom into the person's heart. The third strophe (vv. 6-8) is Ben Sira's attempt to define the charism of inspiration, by which the Lord reveals himself in human language. It ends with an interesting phrase, "the law of the Lord's covenant," which shows how well Ben Sira understood the connection of law and covenant: the former comprises the stipulations that the covenant-partners are bound to observe. The last strophe (vv. 9-11) pictures the immortality which Ben Sira augurs for the wise man, and, no doubt, hoped to enjoy himself: it consists solely in perpetual "memory ... name ... praise ..." Apart from that, Ben Sira knew only of the dusty, ghostly oblivion of Sheol.

# X

## HYMN OF PRAISE
### 39:12-35

[12]I have yet more to say, which I have thought upon,
and I am filled, like the moon at the full.
[13]Listen to me, O you holy sons,
and bud like a rose growing by a stream of water;
[14]send forth fragrance like frankincense,
and put forth blossoms like a lily.
Scatter the fragrance, and sing a hymn of praise;
bless the Lord for all his works;
[15]ascribe majesty to his name
and give thanks to him with praise,
with songs on your lips, and with lyres;
and this you shall say in thanksgiving:
[16]"All things are the works of the Lord,
for they are very good,
and whatever he commands will be done in his time."
[17]No one can say, "What is this?"
"Why is that?"
for in God's time all things will be sought after.

At his word the waters stood in a heap,
   and the reservoirs of water at the word of his mouth.
[18]At his command whatever pleases him is done,
   and none can limit his saving power.
[19]The works of all flesh are before him,
   and nothing can be hid from his eyes.
[20]From everlasting to everlasting he beholds them,
   and nothing is marvelous to him.
[21]No one can say, "What is this?"
      "Why is that?"
   for everything has been created for its use.
[22]His blessing covers the dry land like a river,
   and drenches it like a flood.
[23]The nations will incur his wrath,
   just as he turns fresh water into salt.
[24]To the holy his ways are straight,
   just as they are obstacles to the wicked.
[25]From the beginning good things
      were created for good people,
   just as evil things for sinners.
[26]Basic to all the needs of man's life
   are water and fire and iron and salt
and wheat flour and milk and honey,
   the blood of the grape, and oil and clothing.
[27]All these are for good to the godly,
   just as they turn into evils for sinners.
[28]There are winds that have been created for vengeance,
   and in their anger they scourge heavily;
in the time of consummation they
      will pour out their strength
   and calm the anger of their Maker.
[29]Fire and hail and famine and pestilence,
   all these have been created for vengeance;
[30]the teeth of wild beasts, and scorpions and vipers,
   and the sword that punishes the
      ungodly with destruction;
[31]they will rejoice in his commands,
      and be made ready on earth for their service,
      and when their times come

they will not transgress his word.
32Therefore from the beginning I have been convinced,
and have thought this out and left it in writing:
33The works of the Lord are all good,
and he will supply every need in its hour.
34And no one can say, "This is worse than that,"
for all things will prove good in their season.
35So now sing praise with all your heart and voice,
and bless the name of the Lord.


This fine composition, similar to 16:24-17:14, combines the basic structure of a hymn or psalm of praise with typical sapiential discussion about divine providence and human life. The structure, often exemplified in the Psalter, consists in a summons, addressed usually to a group, to utter God's praise, followed by reasons or motives why he deserves to be praised. The main point here seems to be that everything has been created for a purpose, to reward the good, or punish the wicked, or both. The summons is in vv. 13-15, the motives in vv. 16-34. 13-14 are reminiscent of chap. 24 with its images of blossom and fruit and perfume. In vv. 16-21 Ben Sira expatiates on the work of creation; from Gen 1 he echoes the stress on the goodness of each thing made, drawing attention to the Creator's wisdom in providing for every need. 17 may refer to the separation of waters above from waters below, Gen 1:7. In vv. 22-25 he introduces an important distinction: though everything created is good, still many things may act disastrously to punish the wicked. Verse 25 sums up this idea, and v. 27 repeats it. In vv. 28-30 other examples are given. In v. 32 Ben Sira comes forward with a personal conclusion, rather strange in a hymn. 33-34 are another summary, and v. 35 repeats the summons of v. 15.

## HUMANITY'S UNHAPPY LOT
## 40:1-10

**40**  Much labor was created for every man,
  and a heavy yoke is upon the sons of Adam,
from the day they come forth from their mother's womb
  to the day they return to the mother of all.
[2]Their perplexities and fear of heart —
  their anxious thought is the day of death,
[3]from the man who sits on a splendid throne
  to the one who is humbled in dust and ashes,
[4]from the man who wears purple and a crown
  to the one who is clothed in burlap;
[5]there is anger and envy and trouble and unrest,
  and fear of death, and fury and strife.
And when one rests upon his bed,
  his sleep at night confuses his mind.
[6]He gets little or no rest,
  and afterward in his sleep, as though
    he were on watch,
he is troubled by the visions of his mind
  like one who has escaped from the battle-front;
[7]at the moment of his rescue he wakes up,
  and wonders that his fear came to nothing.
[8]With all flesh, both man and beast,
  and upon sinners seven times more,
[9]are death and bloodshed and strife and sword,
  calamities, famine and affliction and plague.
[10]All these were created for the wicked,
  and on their account the flood came.

Quite abruptly Ben Sira turns to a rather pessimistic
account of some unhappy experiences common to all "sons
of Adam." Verse 1d, "the mother of all" is of course
"Mother Earth," cf. Ps 139:15. The unity of humankind is
stressed: whether kings or paupers, in these afflictions the
whole race is kin. Their "heavy yoke" is not due to physical

toil or disease; it is strictly psychological — perplexities, fear, anxious thought, etc., as in vv. 2 and 5, not only by day but by night as well. So much is common to all; but Ben Sira reminds us that sinners will suffer "seven times more" the physical disasters of v. 9.

## CONTRAST OF SINNERS AND JUST
### 40:11-17

[11] All things that are from the earth
     turn back to the earth,
 and what is from the waters
     returns to the sea.
[12] All bribery and injustice will be blotted out,
     but good faith will stand for ever.
[13] The wealth of the unjust will dry up like a torrent,
     and crash like a loud clap of thunder in a rain.
[14] A generous man will be made glad;
     likewise transgressors will utterly fail.
[15] The children of the ungodly will
     not put forth many branches;
 they are unhealthy roots upon sheer rock.
[16] The reeds by any water or river bank
     will be plucked up before any grass.
[17] Kindness is like a garden of blessings,
     and almsgiving endures for ever.

Verse 11b is another small mistake by the Greek translator: Ben Sira wrote "and what is from on high returns on high," meaning not the soul but the breath of life, which the Lord gives and then takes back. Cf. Gen 2:7, Ps 104:29f., Eccles 12:7. 12 and 17 stress the permanence of goodness; evil may be frightening, like a flash flood (vv. 13f.), but will soon cease.

## COMPARISONS
40:18-27

18Life is sweet for the self-reliant and the worker,
   but he who finds treasure is better off than both.
19Children and the building of a city
      establish a man's name,
   but a blameless wife is accounted better than both.
20Wine and music gladden the heart,
   but the love of wisdom is better than both.
21The flute and the harp make pleasant melody,
   but a pleasant voice is better than both.
22The eye desires grace and beauty,
   but the green shoots of grain more than both.
23A friend or a companion never meets one amiss,
   but a wife with her husband is better than both.
24Brothers and help are for a time of trouble,
   but almsgiving rescues better than both.
25Gold and silver make the foot stand sure,
   but good counsel is esteemed more than both.
26Riches and strength lift up the heart,
   but the fear of the Lord is better than both.
There is no loss in the fear of the Lord.
   and with it there is no need to seek for help.
27The fear of the Lord is like a garden of blessing,
   and covers a man better than any glory.

Ben Sira composes an elaborate series of ten riddles,
reminiscent of the ten beatitudes in 25:7-11. The formula is
"A and B are both good (in some particular way); but better
than either is C." The problem was, given A and B, to name
C. All are blessings from God, but some are more precious
than others. The Greek text here is in disorder: v. 19, for "a
blameless wife" read "the attainment of wisdom," i.e. this is
the best of three ways of "establishing a name." After v. 19
the third comparison has been omitted: insert "Sheepfolds
and orchards bring flourishing health/but better than either
is a devoted wife." In v. 20, "love of wisdom" should read

"love in marriage." 24, almsgiving is preferable to brother or helper because it directly invokes God's blessing; cf. note on 29:20. As we should expect, Ben Sira's climax (vv. 26-27) is "fear of the Lord."

## ON BEGGARY
### 40:28-30

28My son, do not lead the life of a beggar;
  it is better to die than to beg.
29When a man looks to the table of another,
  his existence cannot be considered as life.
He pollutes himself with another man's food,
   but a man who is intelligent and well-instructed
    guards against that.
30In the mouth of the shameless begging is sweet,
  but in his stomach a fire is kindled.

A brief section, of only four couplets, warns against the life of a beggar. How, in a case of bankruptcy or destitution, it was to be avoided, Ben Sira does not explain. He only underlines the bitter shame it must cause to a man of feeling.

## ON DEATH
### 41:1-4

**41**  O death, how bitter is the reminder of you
  to one who lives at peace among his possessions,
to a man without distractions, who
   is prosperous in everything,
  and who still has the vigor to enjoy his food!
2O death, how welcome is your sentence
  to one who is in need and is failing in strength,
very old and distracted over everything;
   to one who is contrary, and has lost his patience!

> [3]Do not fear the sentence of death;
>    remember your former days and the end of life;
>   this is the decree from the Lord for all flesh,
> [4]   and how can you reject the good pleasure
>        of the Most High?
>   Whether life is for ten or a hundred or a thousand years,
>       there is no inquiry about it in Hades.

Ben Sira has already treated of health and illness, and of the death of a friend or relative. Now he invites the reader to a *Memento mori*, meditation on one's own death. With dramatic imagery he addresses Death directly, personifying him as a messenger come to announce the divine sentence: unwelcome to the prosperous, but well-received (in theory at least) by the unfortunate. In vv. 3-4 he suddenly switches his address to his pupil, urging him to resignation and acceptance of what is, after all, a universal fate. 4c, whether one's life was long or short, happy or unhappy, virtuous or vicious, will make no difference in Sheol. Such was the standard older belief, before the development of the doctrine of a judgment after death.

## SINNERS PUNISHED IN THEIR OFFSPRING
41:5-13

> [5]The children of sinners are abominable children,
>    and they frequent the haunts of the ungodly.
> [6]The inheritance of the children of sinners will perish,
>    and on their posterity will be a perpetual reproach.
> [7]Children will blame an ungodly father,
>    for they suffer reproach because of him.
> [8]Woe to you, ungodly men,
>    who have forsaken the law of the Most High God!
> [9]When you are born, you are born to a curse;

and when you die, a curse is your lot.
¹⁰Whatever is from the dust returns to dust;
   so the ungodly go from curse to destruction.
¹¹The mourning of men is about their bodies,
   but the evil name of sinners will be blotted out.
¹²Have regard for your name, since it will remain for you
   longer than a thousand great stores of gold.
¹³The days of a good life are numbered,
 _ but a good name endures for ever.

Ben Sira believes however that there is a great difference in this life between the just and the unjust. It consists in the bad reputation the latter leave behind them, the bad character of their children, and the calamity that is sure to light on these children, in view of their parents' sins. The argument may seem weak to a modern reader. Already it had been bluntly rejected in the book of Job (21:19-21):

"You say, 'God stores up their iniquity for their sons.'
Let him recompense it to themselves, that they may know it.
Let their own eyes see their destruction,
   and let them drink of the wrath of the Almighty.
For what do they care for their houses after them,
   when the number of their months is cut off?"

Verse 8 shows that Ben Sira is thinking of apostate Jews who make no attempt to observe the Mosaic law; practically, they have become pagans and idolaters; cf. above, 2:12-14. Verse 10 still refers to these apostates; we might be inclined to ask the author if things are any different for the virtuous, who also "return to dust." But of course he would reply that they leave behind them virtuous children and a good name.

# TRUE AND FALSE SHAME
## 41:14-42:8

[14]My children, observe instruction and be at peace...
[16]Therefore show respect for my words:
For it is not good to retain every kind of shame,
    and not everything is confidently
        esteemed by every one.
[17]Be ashamed of immorality, before your father or
        mother;
    and of a lie, before a prince or ruler;
[18]of a transgression, before a judge or magistrate;
    and of iniquity, before a congregation or the people;
of unjust dealing, before your partner or friend;
[19]    and of theft, in the place where you live.
Be ashamed before the truth of God and his covenant.
    Be ashamed of selfish behavior at meals,
of surliness in receiving and giving,
[20]    and of silence, before those who greet you;
of looking at a woman who is a harlot,
[21]    and of rejecting the appeal of a kinsman;
of taking away some one's portion or gift,
    and of gazing at another man's wife;
[22]of meddling with his maidservant —
    and do not approach her bed;
of abusive words, before friends —
    and do not upbraid after making a gift;
[23]of repeating and telling what you hear,
    and of revealing secrets.
Then you will show proper shame,
    and will find favor with every man.
**42** Of the following things do not be ashamed,
    and do not let partiality lead you to sin:
[2]of the law of the Most High and his covenant,
    and of rendering judgment to acquit the ungodly;
[3]of keeping accounts with a partner
    or with traveling companions,
    and of dividing the inheritance of friends;

4of accuracy with scales and weights,
  and of acquiring much or little;
5of profit from dealing with merchants,
  and of much discipline of children,
  and of whipping a wicked servant severely.
6Where there is an evil wife, a seal is a good thing;
  and where there are many hands, lock things up.
7Whatever you deal out, let it be by number and weight,
  and make a record of all that you give out or take in.
8Do not be ashamed to instruct the stupid or foolish
  or the aged man who quarrels with the young.
Then you will be truly instructed,
  and will be approved before all men.

Back in 4:20-28 Ben Sira had already attempted a discrimination between two opposite senses of the word *bosheth,* "shame." He now treats the question systematically. 14a, 16, are an introduction addressed to "my sons." (14b-15 are from 20:30f., and out of place here.) In vv. 17-23 twenty actions are listed which one should be ashamed to commit — often before specified witnesses whose disapproval would surely be wounding to one's self-esteem. In 42:1-8 is a corresponding list of sixteen praiseworthy actions one should *not* be ashamed of performing. (RSV does not give the numbers exactly.) Yet they are such as might cause embarrassment or hesitation, for fear of seeming harsh or suspicious or too meticulous. Ben Sira encourages his young hearers not to be deterred by human respect from due precautions and even severity. The first set of eight (vv. 2-5a) are concerned with business dealings; the second (vv. 5b-8), with control and direction of a household.

## WORRY OVER A DAUGHTER
42:9-14

9A daughter keeps her father secretly wakeful,
  and worry over her robs him of sleep;

when she is young, lest she do not marry,
     or if married, lest she be hated;
10while a virgin, lest she be defiled
     or become pregnant in her father's house;
or having a husband, lest she prove unfaithful,
     or, though married, lest she be barren.
11Keep strict watch over a headstrong daughter,
     lest she make you a laughingstock to your enemies,
a byword in the city and notorious among the people,
     and put you to shame before the great multitude.
12Do not look upon any one for beauty,
     and do not sit in the midst of women;
13for from garments comes the moth,
     and from a woman comes woman's wickedness.
14Better is the wickedness of a man
          than a woman who does good;
     and it is a woman who brings shame and disgrace.

These ten couplets show Ben Sira's misogyny at its worst. The unfortunate girl is presumed to be unwise, therefore prone to every temptation and weakness. Her own good or advantage is not considered; Ben Sira's concern is entirely with the father's reputation. Verses 12 and 14 are uncertain translations.

# XI

## THE WORKS OF GOD
42:15-43:33

This section is Ben Sira's longest and most elaborate hymn to the Lord of nature.

### God's Wisdom
42:15-25

15I will now call to mind the works of the Lord,
  and will declare what I have seen.
By the words of the Lord his works are done.
16The sun looks down on everything with its light,
  and the work of the Lord is full of his glory.
17The Lord has not enabled his holy ones
  to recount all his marvelous works,
which the Lord the Almighty has established
  that the universe may stand firm in his glory.
18He searches out the abyss, and the hearts of men,
  and considers their crafty devices.
For the Most High knows all that may be known,
  and he looks into the signs of the age.
19He declares what has been and what is to be,
  and he reveals the tracks of hidden things.

[20]No thought escapes him,
  and not one word is hidden from him.
[21]He has ordained the splendors of his wisdom,
  and he is from everlasting and to everlasting.
Nothing can be added or taken away,
  and he needs no one to be his counselor.
[22]How greatly to be desired are all his works,
  and how sparkling they are to see!
[23]All these things live and remain for ever
  for every need, and are all obedient.
[24]All things are twofold, one opposite the other,
  and he has made nothing incomplete.
[25]One confirms the good things of the other,
  and who can have enough of beholding his glory?

In three strophes (vv. 15-17, 18-21b, 21c-25) Ben Sira praises the omnipotence and wisdom of the Creator. The first strophe refers to his "works" (three times) and "glory." 17, even his "holy ones" (= angels) cannot adequately describe his marvels; how much less a man or woman, however wise! The second strophe is on his omniscience. The third praises the beauty of creation, particularly in the harmonious combination of such varied creatures.

Wonders of Sky and Ocean
43:1-26

**43** The pride of the heavenly heights is the clear
    firmament
  the appearance of heaven in a spectacle of glory.
[2]The sun, when it appears, making proclamation as it
    goes forth,
  is a marvelous instrument, the
    work of the Most High.
[3]At noon it parches the land;
  and who can withstand its burning heat?
[4]A man tending a furnace works in burning heat,
  but the sun burns the mountains three times as much;
it breathes out fiery vapors,
  and with bright beams it blinds the eyes.

5 Great is the Lord who made it;
   and at his command it hastens on its course.
6 He made the moon also, to serve in its season
   to mark the times and to be an everlasting sign.
7 From the moon comes the sign for feast days,
   a light that wanes when it has reached the full.
8 The month is named for the moon,
   increasing marvelously in its phases,
an instrument of the hosts on high
   shining forth in the firmament of heaven.
9 The glory of the stars is the beauty of heaven,
   a gleaming array in the heights of the Lord.
10 At the command of the Holy One they stand as ordered,
   they never relax in their watches.
11 Look upon the rainbow, and praise him who made it,
   exceedingly beautiful in its brightness.
12 It encircles the heaven with its glorious arc;
   the hands of the Most High have stretched it out.
13 By his command he sends the driving snow
   and speeds the lightnings of his judgment.
14 Therefore the storehouses are opened,
   and the clouds fly forth like birds.
15 In his majesty he amasses the clouds,
   and the hailstones are broken in pieces.
16 At his appearing the mountains are shaken;
   at his will the south wind blows.
17 The voice of his thunder rebukes the earth;
   so do the tempest from the north and the whirlwind.
He scatters the snow like birds flying down,
   and its descent is like locusts alighting.
18 The eye marvels at the beauty of its whiteness,
   and the mind is amazed at its falling.
19 He pours the hoarfrost upon the earth like salt,
   and when it freezes, it becomes pointed thorns.
20 The cold north wind blows,
   and ice freezes over the water;
it rests upon every pool of water,
   and the water puts it on like a breastplate.

21 He consumes the mountains
       and burns up the wilderness,
       and withers the tender grass like fire.
22 A mist quickly heals all things;
       when the dew appears, it refreshes from the heat.
23 By his counsel he stilled the great deep
       and planted islands in it.
24 Those who sail the sea tell of its dangers,
       and we marvel at what we hear.
25 For in it are strange and marvelous works,
       all kinds of living things, and huge creatures of the sea.
26 Because of him his messenger finds the way,
       and by his word all things hold together.

After the general treatment in the preceding section, Ben Sira comes to consider in detail heavenly bodies and the weather phenomena which were thought to depend on them. First, the firmament itself; next the sun, vv. 2-5, and the moon, vv. 6-8, a calendar-marker as in Gen 1:14. 8, the name for the new moon was *hodesh,* which also means "month." 9-10 praise the stars because although they steadily revolve each night they do not (like the moon) wax and wane, nor (like the sun) rise and set. 11-12, on the rainbow, underline its symbolism as the bow which the Lord has bent but will never again shoot at the earth (Gen 9:13-16). 13-17b deal with thunder storms as evidence of the Lord's wondrous power; 17c-20 with winter storms, which bring dazzling snow and ice. 21-22 describe rain storms which relieve drought or heat wave. Finally, vv. 23-26, Ben Sira cites the element regarded by the Jews of his time as the most alien and menacing: the sea. Yet this too is under the Lord's control.


Summons to Praise
43:27-33

27 Though we speak much we cannot reach the end,
       and the sum of our words is: "He is the all."
28 Where shall we find strength to praise him?

For he is greater than all his works.

29 Terrible is the Lord and very great,
and marvelous is his power.

30 When you praise the Lord, exalt him as much as you
can;
for he will surpass even that.

When you exalt him, put forth all your strength,
and do not grow weary, for you cannot praise him
enough.

31 Who has seen him and can describe him?
Or who can extol him as he is?

32 Many things greater than these lie hidden,
for we have seen but few of his works.

33 For the Lord has made all things,
and to the godly he has granted wisdom.

In the conclusion of the great hymn Ben Sira again confesses the inability of humans to praise the Lord as he deserves. Verse 27 uses a formula which might sound Stoic or pantheistic: lit., "He is all." But the whole context excludes any confusion of the Lord with his creation; he remains distinct from all creatures just because he transcends them, and v. 28 is a grandiose declaration of that transcendence. 33, Ben Sira concludes with a reminder of the connection between wisdom and "godliness"; the former is the Lord's gift to those who practise the latter.

# XII

## PRAISE OF THE ANCESTORS
44:1-49:16

This is perhaps the best known section of Ben Sira's wisdom manual. He intends it as a parallel to the preceding praise of the Creator at work in the world of nature, which presented traditional creation theology. Now he proceeds to the divine activity in the world of history, which is specifically Israelite, and may be called salvation theology. He fully justifies his claim to long study and close familiarity with the wisdom of his predecessors and all the sacred writings and traditions of his people; cf. 24:28-31, 39:1-3, besides the testimony of his grandson in the Prologue. He is familiar with almost the entire body of canonical Jewish scriptures as we know them today. Only Ruth, Esther and the Canticle are missing, and Ezra is not mentioned; the book of Daniel of course was published later. One interesting change is that while his sources are largely in prose (Pentateuch, historical books) he summarizes their contents in dignified and expressive poetry. This Bible history is one in a long series of similar outlines or summaries. Perhaps the earliest form was the prose "confession" associated with covenant renewal or the offering of first fruits. For the former, cf. Jos 24:1-13; for the latter, Deut 26:5-9. Three of the Psalms, 78, 105, 106, expand the history in poetic form.

Ezekiel had reviewed pre-exilic history in the form of an allegory, in Ezek 16 and 23, and in plain terms in Ezek 20. A similar passage is Ezra's prayer in Neh 9:7-37. All of these are religious histories, not political or social; they treat of the covenant relationship between the Lord and the people of Israel. This has two aspects: the faithfulness of the Lord to the covenant, and the unfaithfulness of Israel to the same. For the former cp. Ps 105; for the latter, Pss 78, 106.

Ben Sira's "Bible history" naturally influenced his successors. Wisdom of Solomon, chap. 10, reviews the history of the patriarchs, then devotes eight chapters to a midrash on the Exodus. 1 Mac 2:51-60 has a brief poetic version. Finally, it influenced the great paean on faith in Heb 11.

## Introduction
### 44:1-15

**44** Let us now praise famous men,
    and our fathers in their generations.
[2]The Lord apportioned to them great glory,
    his majesty from the beginning.
[3]There were those who ruled in their kingdoms,
    and were men renowned for their power,
giving counsel by their understanding,
    and proclaiming prophecies;
[4]leaders of the people in their deliberations
    and in understanding of learning for the people,
        wise in their words of instruction;
[5]those who composed musical tunes
    and set forth verses in writing;
[6]rich men furnished with resources,
    living peaceably in their habitations —
[7]all these were honored in their generations,
    and were the glory of their times.
[8]There are some of them who have left a name,
    so that men declare their praise.
[9]And there are some who have no memorial,
    who have perished as though they had not lived;

they have become as though they had not been born,
   and so have their children after them.
[10]But these were men of mercy,
   whose righteous deeds have not been forgotten;
[11]their prosperity will remain with their descendants,
   and their inheritance to their children's children.
[12]Their descendants stand by the covenants;
   their children also, for their sake.
[13]Their posterity will continue for ever,
   and their glory will not be blotted out.
[14]Their bodies were buried in peace,
   and their name lives to all generations.
[15]Peoples will declare their wisdom,
   and the congregation proclaims their praise.

Ben Sira solemnly announces his theme, in the singular: "Let me now ..." "Famous men" is lit. "men of *hesed*" = "who are loyal to the covenant." The verb "to praise" is regularly applied in the liturgy to praise of the Lord, but here Ben Sira applies it to human beings, the great religious heroes of the past, with the very practical aim of motivating his young hearers to similar loyalty. Though here he speaks only of praise, in fact he will pass some severe negative judgments; see below on 47:19f. Verses 3-6 distribute the people referred to in twelve classes, which in the original are intended to be all distinct, not synonymous as RSV makes them. The distinction in vv. 8-9 has been misunderstood: for Ben Sira, to leave no "name" behind at death is to be completely extinct, and naturally he cannot commemorate exploits and virtues of which — though they really happened — no record now exists. Verse 9 states this quite clearly. In v. 10, "these" refers, *not* to the forgotten men of v. 9 but to the well-remembered ones of v. 8. Verses 11-15 underline the immortality conferred on them by descendants and fame. In v. 15, their virtues are summed up as "wisdom." 15b is in the Hebrew the same phrase as in 31:11b, with "their" in place of "his."

## Enoch and Noah
### 44:16-18

> [16]Enoch pleased the Lord, and was taken up;
>   he was an example of repentance to all generations.
> [17]Noah was found perfect and righteous;
>   in the time of wrath he was taken in exchange;
> therefore a remnant was left to the earth
>   when the flood came.
> [18]Everlasting covenants were made with him
>   that all flesh should not be blotted out by a flood.

This brief section mentions only two characters from Gen 1-11. Even Enoch's presence is doubtful, since he will reappear in 49:14. In the Hebrew Ben Sira calls him "a sign (or example) of knowledge"; the Greek translator changed this to "repentance." Neither attribute is mentioned in Gen 5:24, where we read "Enoch walked with God; and he was not, for God took him." But for Ben Sira any familiarity with divine things can be understood as wisdom, and the being taken was interpreted as "assumption" into the heavenly court. The Letter to the Hebrews (11:5-9) lists the same names as here in the same order, from Enoch through to Jacob. Enoch and his fate became the focus of much speculation, and many apocryphal writings, extending into the Christian era, were placed under his name. V. 17, Ben Sira cites the prophetic theme of "remnant"; cf. Amos 5:15, Isa 10:19-22.

## Abraham, Isaac, Jacob
### 44:19-23

> [19]Abraham was the great father of a multitude of nations,
>   and no one has been found like him in glory;
> [20]he kept the law of the Most High,
>   and was taken into covenant with him;
> he established the covenant in his flesh,
>   and when he was tested he was found faithful.
> [21]Therefore the Lord assured him by an oath
>   that the nations would be blessed through his posterity;

that he would multiply him like the dust of the earth,
  and exalt his posterity like the stars,
and cause them to inherit from sea to sea
  and from the River to the ends of the earth.
22To Isaac also he gave the same assurance
  for the sake of Abraham his father.
23The blessing of all men and the covenant
  he made to rest upon the head of Jacob;
he acknowledged him with his blessings,
  and gave him his inheritance;
he determined his portions,
  and distributed them among twelve tribes.

The second group includes the three patriarchs, along with the sons of Jacob-Israel as eponyms of the twelve tribes. Verse 20 alludes to four outstanding merits on the part of Abraham: he observed the Law, he made a covenant with the Lord, he was circumcised, he was ready even to offer his son Isaac in sacrifice. The first of these is a clear anachronism (Abraham having lived centuries before Moses), but was a popular belief at that time and later; along with the third point it was of vital importance for the survival of Judaism in Ben Sira's time. Cf. 1 Mac 1:48f. Of interest here is the way Ben Sira has reversed the order of events in Genesis. There, God first calls Abraham and promises to bless him (Gen 12:1-3), then makes a covenant with him (ib. 15:18), before Abraham is circumcised (ib. 17:24f) or proves his fidelity in the great test (ib. 22). In other words, Ben Sira seems to be implying that blessing and covenant were a reward for Abraham's merits and good works. Verse 21, in a kind of response, lists three promises sworn to by the Lord. The third ("cause them to inherit . . .") exaggerates the terms of Genesis, where God promises only the land of Canaan; cf. Gen 12:7, 13:14f., 15:18, 17:8. Ben Sira here quotes the standard expression of universal royal rule, from Ps 72:8 and Zech 9:10, and transfers it from the line of David to the entire posterity of Abraham. "From sea to sea" means from the Persian Gulf to the Mediterranean; the river is the Euphrates. He says nothing about the deception practised by Jacob on his father and older brother, by which he acquired the blessing and the inheritance (Gen 27); instead he makes a smooth transition in v. 23 from the individual to the group, divided into tribes. Cf. 45:5, where the people alone is meant.

Moses
45:1-5

> **45** From his descendants the Lord brought forth a man
> of mercy,
>   who found favor in the sight of all flesh
> and was beloved by God and man,
>   Moses, whose memory is blessed.
> ²He made him equal in glory to the holy ones,
>   and made him great in the fears of his enemies.
> ³By his words he caused signs to cease;
>   the Lord glorified him in the presence of kings.
> He gave him commands for his people,
>   and showed him part of his glory.
> ⁴He sanctified him through faithfulness and meekness;
>   he chose him out of all mankind.
> ⁵He made him hear his voice,
>   and led him into the thick darkness,
> and gave him the commandments face to face,
>   the law of life and knowledge,
> to teach Jacob the covenant,
>   and Israel his judgments.

It is strange that Ben Sira here omits all mention of Joseph, who surely was a man of *hesed* and an exemplar of wisdom; he is brought in merely as an afterthought in 49:15. Instead, passing over the later chapters of Genesis, he proceeds to comment on Exodus. First naturally is Moses, whose career is outlined in nine couplets, which recall his confrontation with Pharaoh, his face-to-face contacts with the Lord, his mediatorship of law and covenant. In view of the identification of law with wisdom we might have expected more development of Moses' role; but in fact he serves mainly to introduce the much longer eulogy of his "brother" Aaron.

## Aaron
## 45:6-22

[6]He exalted Aaron, the brother of Moses,
   a holy man like him, of the tribe of Levi.
[7]He made an everlasting covenant with him,
   and gave him the priesthood of the people.
He blessed him with splendid vestments,
      and put a glorious robe upon him.
[8]He clothed him with superb perfection,
   and strengthened him with the symbols of authority,
   the linen breeches, the long robe, and the ephod.
[9]And he encircled him with pomegranates,
   with very many golden bells round about,
to send forth a sound as he walked,
   to make their ringing heard in the temple
   as a reminder to the sons of his people;
[10]with a holy garment, of gold and blue
   and purple, the work of an embroiderer;
with the oracle of judgment, Urim and Thummim;
[11]   with twisted scarlet, the work of a craftsman;
with precious stones engraved like signets,
   in a setting of gold, the work of a jeweler,
for a reminder, in engraved letters,
   according to the number of the tribes of Israel;
[12]with a gold crown upon his turban,
   inscribed like a signet with "Holiness,"
a distinction to be prized, the work of an expert,
   the delight of the eyes, richly adorned.
[13]Before his time there never were such beautiful things.
      No outsider ever put them on,
but only his sons
   and his descendants perpetually.
[14]His sacrifices shall be wholly burned
   twice every day continually.
[15]Moses ordained him,

and anointed him with holy oil;
it was an everlasting covenant for him
    and for his descendants all the days of heaven,
to minister to the Lord and serve as priest
    and bless his people in his name.
[16]He chose him out of all the living
    to offer sacrifice to the Lord,
incense and a pleasing odor as a memorial portion,
    to make atonement for the people.
[17]In his commandments he gave him
    authority in statutes and judgments,
to teach Jacob the testimonies,
    and to enlighten Israel with his law.
[18]Outsiders conspired against him,
    and envied him in the wilderness,
Dathan and Abiram and their men
    and the company of Korah, in wrath and anger.
[19]The Lord saw it and was not pleased,
    and in the wrath of his anger they were destroyed;
he wrought wonders against them
    to consume them in flaming fire.
[20]He added glory to Aaron
    and gave him a heritage;
he allotted to him the first of the first fruits,
    he prepared bread of first fruits in abundance;
[21]for they eat the sacrifices to the Lord,
    which he gave to him and his descendants.
[22]But in the land of the people he has no inheritance,
    and he has no portion among the people;
    for the Lord himself is his portion and inheritance.

To Ben Sira it is the cult, the public "service" of Israel's God, that constitutes the crowning glory of religion. But this cult is by no means separated from wisdom or from the law. Aaron's responsibilities include *torah,* instruction — we might call it catechism — which is clearly dependent on wisdom (45:17, cf. 5). The latter is just as much involved in the cult as in the observances of family, social and commercial life. Ben Sira devotes three strophes (vv. 8-9, 10-11,

12-13) to the vestments of the high priest, following Ex 28 and 39. Without technical details, he expresses his delight in the visual beauty of these adornments. In v. 15 comes the second mention of a covenant — that with Aaron, founded on his anointing. He is, then, a Messiah, or according to the English equivalent of this Hebrew word, an anointed one; there is here a connection with the community of Qumran which a century or so later were expecting a messiah "of Aaron" as well as a messiah "of Israel." 15ef, "to minister to the Lord ... and bless his people" is a neat summary of priestly duties, expanded in vv. 16-17.

### Phinehas and Other Priests
### 45:23-26

23Phinehas the son of Eleazar is the third in glory,
     for he was zealous in the fear of the Lord,
and stood fast, when the people turned away,
     in the ready goodness of his soul,
     and made atonement for Israel.
24Therefore a covenant of peace
         was established with him,
     that he should be leader of the sanctuary
         and of his people,
that he and his descendants should have
     the dignity of the priesthood for ever.
25A covenant was also established with David,
     the son of Jesse, of the tribe of Judah:
the heritage of the king is from son to son only;
     so the heritage of Aaron is for his descendants.
26May the Lord grant you wisdom in your heart
     to judge his people in righteousness,
so that their prosperity may not vanish,
     and that their glory may endure
         throughout their generations.

The third great pioneer after Moses and Aaron is Phinehas, whose dramatic intervention to vindicate the Law is narrated in Num 25:6-13, and alluded to elsewhere. Like his grandfather Aaron he glories in a special covenant, i.e. a divine blessing accorded to him and his descendants, by which (so Ben Sira believed) they should exercise the priesthood in perpetuity. Verse 25 means to contrast the Davidic covenant with that of Phinehas: the former affects only one person in each generation, but the latter is for all his descendants. In v. 26 Ben Sira suddenly addresses them, his contemporaries. As rulers of the people they have inherited not only the priestly office but the responsibilities of the kings as well; hence the blessing he asks for them does not concern the cult but government. It is what Solomon had prayed for (1 Kgs 3:9-12), wisdom in the heart, to govern people with justice. Ben Sira may already have had a premonition of the harm to be caused a few years later by the unscrupulous personal rivalries of claimants to the high-priesthood; cf. 2 Mac 4.

Joshua, Caleb, the Judges
46:1-12

**46** Joshua the son of Nun was mighty in war,
and was the successor of Moses in prophesying.
He became, in accordance with his name,
a great savior of God's elect,
to take vengeance on the enemies
that rose against them,
so that he might give Israel its inheritance.
²How glorious he was when he lifted his hands
and stretched out his sword against the cities!
³Who before him ever stood so firm?
For he waged the wars of the Lord.
⁴Was not the sun held back by his hand?
And did not one day become as long as two?
⁵He called upon the Most High, the Mighty One,
when enemies pressed him on every side,
⁶and the great Lord answered him
with hailstones of mighty power.
He hurled down war upon that nation,

and at the descent of Beth-horon
  he destroyed those who resisted,
so that the nations might know his armament,
  that he was fighting in the sight of the Lord;
  for he wholly followed the Mighty One.
[7]And in the days of Moses he did a loyal deed,
  he and Caleb the son of Jephunneh:
they withstood the congregation,
  restrained the people from sin,
  and stilled their wicked murmuring.
[8]And these two alone were preserved out of
  six hundred thousand people on foot,
to bring them into their inheritance,
  into a land flowing with milk and honey.
[9]And the Lord gave Caleb strength,
  which remained with him to old age,
so that he went up to the hill country,
  and his children obtained it for an inheritance;
[10]so that all the sons of Israel might see
  that it is good to follow the Lord.
[11]The judges also, with their respective names,
  those whose hearts did not fall into idolatry
  and who did not turn away from the Lord—
  may their memory be blessed!
[12]May their bones revive from where they lie,
  and may the name of those who have been honored
  live again in their sons!

Leaving the Pentateuch, Ben Sira proceeds to the books of Joshua and Judges. From them he selects only two figures, Joshua and Caleb, and adds a reference to the Judges as a group. It is remarkable that he gives Joshua more space than Moses; the latter had nine couplets, the former has eleven to himself (46:1-6), and shares four more (vv. 7-8) with Caleb. Verse 1cd, Joshua's name means "Yahweh is salvation"; in Greek it is *Yesous,* Jesus. It was Ben Sira's own personal name. Verses 2-8 summarize the victories narrated in Jos 6-11. Verses 11-12, Ben Sira distinguishes faithful judges from unfaithful, and applies this sacred history to his own time in the form of a prayer: "May their bones revive!" — not by literal resurrection but in the meaning, "God send us such leaders today!" He repeats the formula in 49:10 about the Minor Prophets.

Samuel
46:13-20

[13]Samuel, beloved by his Lord,
  a prophet of the Lord, established the kingdom
  and anointed rulers over his people.
[14]By the law of the Lord he judged the congregation,
  and the Lord watched over Jacob.
[15]By his faithfulness he was proved to be a prophet,
  and by his words he became known
    as a trustworthy seer.
[16]He called upon the Lord, the Mighty One,
  when his enemies pressed him on every side,
    and he offered in sacrifice a sucking lamb.
[17]Then the Lord thundered from heaven,
  and made his voice heard with a mighty sound;
[18]and he wiped out the leaders of the people of Tyre
  and all the rulers of the Philistines.
[19]Before the time of his eternal sleep,
  Samuel called men to witness
    before the Lord and his anointed:
"I have not taken any one's property,
    not so much as a pair of shoes."
  And no man accused him.
[20]Even after he had fallen asleep he prophesied
  and revealed to the king his death,
and lifted up his voice out of the earth in prophecy,
  to blot out the wickedness of the people.

In 12 couplets Samuel is presented as prophet, judge, priest and founder of the kingdom, since he anointed first Saul and then David. Saul is not named, but referred to as "ruler" and "king."

Three episodes from Samuel's career are cited: his symbolic victory over the Philistines, vv. 16-18 (1 Sam 7:9-10);

his farewell discourse, v. 19 (1 Sam 12); the episode of the witch of Endor, v. 20 (1 Sam 28:3-20).

## Nathan and David
## 47:1-11

**47** And after him Nathan rose up
to prophesy in the days of David.
[2]As the fat is selected from the peace offering,
so David was selected from the sons of Israel.
[3]He played with lions as with young goats,
and with bears as with lambs of the flock.
[4]In his youth did he not kill a giant,
and take away reproach from the people,
when he lifted his hand with a stone in the sling
and struck down the boasting of Goliath?
[5]For he appealed to the Lord, the Most High,
and he gave him strength in his right hand
to slay a man mighty in war,
to exalt the power of his people.
[6]So they glorified him for his ten thousands,
and praised him for the blessings of the Lord,
when the glorious diadem was bestowed upon him.
[7]For he wiped out his enemies on every side,
and annihilated his adversaries the Philistines;
he crushed their power even to this day.
[8]In all that he did he gave thanks
to the Holy One, the Most High,
with ascriptions of glory;
he sang praise with all his heart,
and he loved his Maker.
[9]He placed singers before the altar,
to make sweet melody with their voices.
[10]He gave beauty to the feasts,
and arranged their times throughout the year,
while they praised God's holy name,
and the sanctuary resounded from early morning.
[11]The Lord took away his sins,
and exalted his power for ever;

he gave him the covenant of kings
and a throne of glory in Israel.

With a transitional mention of Nathan as Samuel's successor (an insight proper to Ben Sira), David is introduced. He and Solomon have each 16 couplets. The portrait of David is a balanced one, drawn from 2 Sam as well as from 1 Chron. From the former come the lions and bears, the Goliath story, his military successes and the reference to his sins (1 Sam 17; 2 Sam 8 & 11); from the latter come his organization of the temple liturgy and his skill in sacred music (1 Chron 16 & 23).

Solomon
47:12-22

12After him rose up a wise son
who fared amply because of him;
13Solomon reigned in days of peace,
and God gave him rest on every side,
that he might build a house for his name
and prepare a sanctuary to stand for ever.
14How wise you became in your youth!
You overflowed like a river with understanding.
15Your soul covered the earth,
and you filled it with parables and riddles.
16Your name reached to far-off islands,
and you were loved for your peace.
17For your songs and proverbs and parables,
and for your interpretations, the
countries marveled at you.
18In the name of the Lord God,
who is called the God of Israel,
you gathered gold like tin
and amassed silver like lead.
19But you laid your loins beside women,
and through your body you were
brought into subjection.
20You put a stain upon your honor,
and defiled your posterity,

> so that you brought wrath upon your children
>     and they were grieved at your folly,
> 21so that the sovereignty was divided
>     and a disobedient kingdom arose out of Ephraim.
> 22But the Lord will never give up his mercy,
>     nor cause any of his works to perish;
> he will never blot out the
>         descendants of his chosen one,
>     nor destroy the posterity of him who loved him;
> so he gave a remnant to Jacob,
>     and to David a root of his stock.

We might expect Ben Sira to regard Solomon, traditionally held to be the wisest of kings, as his patron, and hence to omit his failings and present an idealized portrait. This was what was done in Chronicles, and later in the Book of Wisdom. But Ben Sira does not do so. He remains faithful to his sources (including 1 Kgs 11:1-8; cf. also Neh 13:26) and refuses to whitewash Solomon's memory. He specifies that Solomon was favored by God on account of the merits of his father (v. 12); that was why he enjoyed peace, riches and wide renown. His building of the temple and of course his wisdom are emphasized. But Ben Sira goes on to refer to his moral and religious backsliding, though without express mention of his worship of foreign gods; Solomon's "stain" is described simply as submission to his wives (v. 19)! Ben Sira does not say of Solomon, as he did of David (v. 11), that "the Lord took away his sins," but only that in spite of them the Lord maintained his promises to David. Finally, he has given a poignant and dramatic tone to the passage by addressing Solomon's ghost in direct second person discourse (vv. 14-20). In the next chapter he does the same for Elijah.

From here on Ben Sira regularly discriminates between the virtuous and the reprobate, following the judgments of the prophets and the retribution theology of the Deuteronomists. The "Praise of Famous Men," as these chapters are generally labeled, is not by any means unvarying eulogy. It includes some explicit blame of infamous men, and these negative examples are an important part of Ben Sira's message.

## Solomon's Successors
### 47:23-25

23Solomon rested with his fathers,
  and left behind him one of his sons,
ample in folly and lacking in understanding,
  Rehoboam, whose policy caused the people to revolt.
Also Jeroboam the son of Nebat,
    who caused Israel to sin
  and gave to Ephraim a sinful way.
24Their sins became exceedingly many,
  so as to remove them from their land.
25For they sought out every sort of wickedness,
  till vengeance came upon them.

Ben Sira lays the blame for the schism that followed Solomon's death equally on his foolish son Rehoboam and his rival Jeroboam; cf. 1 Kgs 11 and 12. Both are sinners whose criminal folly caused the ruin of their people. "Israel ... Ephraim" refer specifically to the northern kingdom which was destroyed and its population dispersed by the Assyrians in 721 B.C.

## Elijah
### 48:1-11

**48**   Then the prophet Elijah arose like a fire,
  and his word burned like a torch.
2He brought a famine upon them,
  and by his zeal he made them few in number.
3By the word of the Lord he shut up the heavens,
  and also three times brought down fire.
4How glorious you were, O Elijah,
    in your wondrous deeds!
  And who has the right to boast which you have?

5You who raised a corpse from death
  and from Hades, by the word of the Most High;
6who brought kings down to destruction,
  and famous men from their beds;
7who heard rebuke at Sinai
  and judgments of vengeance at Horeb;
8who anointed kings to inflict retribution,
  and prophets to succeed you.
9You who were taken up by a whirlwind of fire,
  in a chariot with horses of fire;
10you who are ready at the
    appointed time, it is written,
  to calm the wrath of God before it breaks out in fury.
to turn the heart of the father to the son,
  and to restore the tribes of Jacob.
11Blessed are those who saw you,
  and those who have been adorned in love;
  for we also shall surely live.

Against that background of human folly Ben Sira places two great prophetic figures whose exploits were recorded and embellished in popular tradition, and included in the book of Kings. The first is Elijah the Tishbite (1 Kgs 17—2 Kgs 2). His notice includes 12 couplets, the number given to Samuel. Ben Sira addresses him directly in 9 couplets, as he did Solomon; but whereas Solomon was blamed Elijah naturally receives only praise. In v. 7 is the first explicit identification of Horeb with Sinai. In v. 10, by the phrase "it is written," Ben Sira explicitly cites Scripture — in this case, the very end of the book of the Minor Prophets, Mal 4:5-6. This is evidence that the book was already completed and accepted as authoritative, in his time. The last phrase of v. 10 is also a quotation, from Isa 49:6. Verse 11 is an uncertain text.

Actions of Elijah, which later rabbinical literature will see as inaugurating the messianic age, are already attributed to him by Ben Sira: to restore Israel, to anoint the elect one, and to intervene at the resurrection of the dead.

Elisha
48:12-14

> [12]It was Elijah who was covered by the whirlwind,
>     and Elisha was filled with his spirit;
> in all his days he did not tremble before any ruler,
>     and no one brought him into subjection.
> [13]Nothing was too hard for him,
>     and when he was dead his body prophesied.
> [14]As in his life he did wonders,
>     so in death his deeds were marvelous.

In just four couplets Ben Sira sums up the wonders ascribed to Elijah's successor. His work also dealt exclusively with the northern kingdom.

People of Israel
48:15-16

> [15]For all this the people did not repent,
>     and they did not forsake their sins,
> till they were carried away captive from their land
>     and were scattered over all the earth;
> the people were left very few in number,
>     but with rulers from the house of David.
> [16]Some of them did what was pleasing to God,
>     but others multiplied sins.

These four couplets sum up the end of the northern kingdom, with a reference back to 47:24, and a contrast with the continuance (for about 135 years) of the kingdom of Judah. In 15 Ben Sira uses a phrase, "were scattered over all the earth," which is not found in 2 Kgs 17 but is taken from the Tower of Babel story, Gen 11:8f. This enlarges the dimensions of the event; it becomes a universalized symbol of punishment inflicted on *hubris* and rebellion. At the end of v. 15 the reference to the house of David picks up the remark in 47:22 about the Lord's mercy; but the succeeding phrase v. 16b, "but others [of the Davidic kings] multiplied sins," prepares for the destruction to be recorded in 49:6.

## Hezekiah and Isaiah
48:17-25

> [17]Hezekiah fortified his city,
>   and brought water into the midst of it;
> he tunneled the sheer rock with iron
>   and built pools for water
> [18]In his days Sennacherib came up,
>   and sent the Rabshakeh;
> he lifted up his hand against Zion
>   and made great boasts in his arrogance.
> [19]Then their hearts were shaken and their hands trembled,
>   and they were in anguish, like women in travail.
> [20]But they called upon the Lord who is merciful,
>   spreading forth their hands toward him;
> and the Holy One quickly heard them from heaven,
>   and delivered them by the hand of Isaiah.
> [21]The Lord smote the camp of the Assyrians,
>   and his angel wiped them out.
> [22]For Hezekiah did what was pleading to the Lord,
>   and he held strongly to the ways of David his father,
> which Isaiah the prophet commanded,
>   who was great and faithful in his vision.
> [23]In his days the sun went backward,
>   and he lengthened the life of the king.
> [24]By the spirit of might he saw the last things,
>   and comforted those who mourned in Zion.
> [25]He revealed what was to occur to the end of time,
>   and the hidden things before they came to pass.

In general Ben Sira follows the editors of the Book of Kings (part of the "Deuteronomic history") in their judgments on the merits and demerits of the Davidic dynasty. They had judged Hezekiah to be one of the good kings, and Ben Sira agrees. But he adds a curiously democratic note to the story of the Assyrian threat to the city: "they," apparently the citizens of Jerusalem, play an active role of intercession before the Lord (48:20), and he answers their prayer. There is no mention of such communal prayer, on this occasion, in Kgs, Chr or Isa, so it must be Ben Sira's own addition. The little section on Isaiah (vv. 23-25) stresses his wonder-working and his foretelling of the future. 24b seems to refer to the middle section of the book of Isaiah (Isa 40-55), and shows that already in Ben Sira's time it was complete as we have it now.

Josiah
49:1-3

**49** The memory of Josiah is like a blending of incense
    prepared by the art of the perfumer;
it is sweet as honey to every mouth,
    and like music at a banquet of wine.
²He was led aright in converting the people,
    and took away the abominations of iniquity.
³He set his heart upon the Lord;
    in the days of wicked men he strengthened godliness.

This is another of the "good" kings, and Ben Sira praises him with a series of his favorite images, incense, perfume, honey, music; but his references are surprisingly vague. He says nothing about the finding of the "Book of the Law," nor of the Deuteronomic reform, nor of the great Passover of the 18th year (2 Kgs 22-23). It is more understandable that he should omit mention of Josiah's unhappy and premature death (2 Kgs 23:29).

Kings of Judah, and Jeremiah
49:4-7

⁴Except David and Hezekiah and Josiah
    they all sinned greatly,
for they forsook the law of the Most High;
    the kings of Judah came to an end;
⁵for they gave their power to others,
    and their glory to a foreign nation,
⁶who set fire to the chosen city of the sanctuary,
    and made her streets desolate,
        according to the word of Jeremiah.

7For they had afflicted him:
   yet he had been consecrated in the womb as prophet,
to pluck up and afflict and destroy,
   and likewise to build and to plant.

In vv. 4-5 Ben Sira writes three couplets condemning — with three honorable exceptions — the kings of Judah. He defines their guilt in one incisive phrase: "they forsook the law of the Most High." This refers especially to two contemporaries of Jeremiah, Johoiakim (609 - 598 B.C.) and Zedekiah (597 - 586). Unlike Hezekiah, who had supported Isaiah, these "afflicted" Jeremiah. Verse 6 alludes to the destruction of Jerusalem and its temple in 586 B.C. But (unlike the dispersal of Israel, 48:15) Ben Sira says nothing about any dispersal of Judah, still less about any exile in Babylonia. For some reason unknown to us he ignores all the references, in 2 Kgs 25 and in Jer 29 and 39-43, to migration and exile. Verse 7 is drawn from the prophetic call of Jeremiah (Jer 1:4-10) and ends with the promise of rebuilding and planting.

The Last Prophets
49:8-10

8It was Ezekiel who saw the vision of glory
   which God showed him above the chariot of the
      cherubim.
9For God remembered his enemies with storm,
   and did good to those who directed their ways aright.
10May the bones of the twelve prophets
   revive from where they lie,
for they comforted the people of Jacob
   and delivered them with confident hope.

Ben Sira cites Ezekiel's grandiose vision of the Lord's chariot-throne; but he does not mention that it occurred "among the exiles by the river Chebar" (Ezek 1:1). In the original Hebrew text, v. 9 reads "He [Ezekiel] also made mention of Job, who maintained all the ways of righteousness"; cf. Ezek 14:14, 20. This was a neat way of including Job, a non-Israelite, in the "praise of our ancestors." Unfortunately the Greek translator misunderstood the verse, and RSV follows him. Verse 10 prays for the renewal of the message of consolation brought by the "Book of the Twelve."

The Rebuilders
49:11-13

> 11 How shall we magnify Zerubbabel?
>    He was like a signet on the right hand,
> 12 and so was Jeshua the son of Jozaduk;
> in their days they built the house
>    and raised a temple holy to the Lord,
>    prepared for everlasting glory.
> 13 The memory of Nehemiah also is lasting;
>    he raised for us the walls that had fallen,
> and set up the gates and bars
>    and rebuilt our ruined houses.

With a rhetorical question to his readers Ben Sira proceeds to extol those who restored the material setting (temple and city) of the cult and community life of the Jews. Zerubbabel and Joshua the priest are prominent in the Books of Haggai and Zechariah; for the "signet ring" cf. Hag 2:23. They directed the reconstruction of the temple, 520-515 B.C. The third great rebuilder is Nehemiah, governor of the province of Judah for many years, who in 444 B.C. restored the walls and gates of Jerusalem and carried through a socio-religious reform. Ben Sira applauds all three, but does not mention that each had to migrate to Jerusalem from a place of exile: the first two from Babylonia, Nehemiah from Persia. He passes over in complete silence the fourth important figure of the Restoration, Ezra the Scribe, famous for the reading of the Law (Neh 8); why, we do not know.

Conclusion
49:14-16

> 14 No one like Enoch has been created on earth,
>    for he was taken up from the earth.

15And no man like Joseph has been born,
    and his bones are cared for.
16Shem and Seth were honored among men,
    and Adam above every living being in the creation.

This brief list is meant to link the end of the story to its beginning in 44:16. Enoch is mentioned again, then Joseph. Finally Ben Sira mentions Adam, closing the circle and marking off this summary of written history from his personal experience in the next chapter.

## THE HIGH PRIEST SIMON
50:1-21

**50**    The leader of his brethren and the pride of his people
    was Simon the high priest, son of Onias,
who in his life repaired the house,
    and in his time fortified the temple.
2He laid the foundations for the high double walls,
    the high retaining walls for the temple enclosure.
3In his days a cistern for water was quarried out,
    a reservoir like the sea in circumference.
4He considered how to save his people from ruin,
    and fortified the city to withstand a siege.
5How glorious he was when the people gathered around
        him
    as he came out of the inner sanctuary!
6Like the morning star among the clouds,
    like the moon when it is full;
7like the sun shining upon the temple of the Most High,
    and like the rainbow gleaming in glorious clouds;
8like roses in the days of the first fruits,
    like lilies by a spring of water,
    like a green shoot on Lebanon on a summer day;
9like fire and incense in the censer,
    like a vessel of hammered gold
    adorned with all kinds of precious stones;
10like an olive tree putting forth its fruit,
    and like a cypress towering in the clouds.

11When he put on his glorious robe
  and clothed himself with superb perfection
and went up to the holy altar,
  he made the court of the sanctuary glorious.
12And when he received the portions
  from the hands of the priests,
  as he stood by the hearth of the altar
with a garland of brethren around him,
  he was like a young cedar on Lebanon;
and they surrounded him like the trunks of palm trees,
13  all the sons of Aaron in their splendor
with the Lord's offering in their hands,
  before the whole congregation of Israel.
14Finishing the service at the altars,
  and arranging the offering to the Most High,
    the Almighty,
15he reached out his hand to the cup
  and poured a libation of the blood of the grape;
he poured it out at the foot of the altar,
  a pleasing odor to the Most High, the King of all.
16Then the sons of Aaron shouted,
  they sounded the trumpets of hammered work,
they made a great noise to be heard
  for remembrance before the Most High.
17Then all the people together made haste
  and fell to the ground upon their faces
  to worship their Lord,
    the Almighty, God Most High.
18And the singers praised him with their voices
  in sweet and full-toned melody.
19And the people besought the Lord Most High
  in prayer before him who is merciful,
till the order of worship of the Lord was ended;
  so they completed his service.
20Then Simon came down, and lifted up his hands
  over the whole congregation of the sons of Israel,
to pronounce the blessing of the Lord with his lips,
  and to glory in his name;

> 21and they bowed down in worship a second time,
> to receive the blessing from the Most High.

This is Simon II, high priest about 219 - 196 B.C.; in Hebrew the name is "Simeon the son of Johanan." He is praised first for his care for the military defence of the city, then more at length (vv. 5-21) for his inspiring and glorious performance of the liturgy (v. 5 echoes 46:2). If "inner sanctuary" (v. 5) means the Holy of Holies, then the following description applies to Yom Kippur, the Day of Atonement, on which day alone the high priest entered it. But if it means the main hall of the temple, then the description is of the regular twice-daily sacrifice cited in 45:14; this seems more likely. Verses 6-10, Ben Sira accumulates twelve images from nature to express the "superb perfection" of the ceremony. 11, the "court of the sanctuary" is the inner courtyard where stood the great altar of holocausts. 14-19, after the burning of the sacrificial carcass a libation was poured, the priests intoned a psalm with accompaniment, the people joined in with loud entreaties. 20-21, the high priest pronounced the blessing (Num 6:22-26), using the sacred name YHWH.

## CONCLUDING PRAYER
50:22-24

> 22And now bless the God of all,
> who in every way does great things;
> who exalts our days from birth,
> and deals with us according to his mercy,
> 23May he give us gladness of heart,
> and grant that peace may be in our days in Israel,
> as in the days of old.
> 24May he entrust to us his mercy!
> And let him deliver us in our days!

RSV gives this text in the form which the Greek translator gave it; Ben Sira's original had been much more specific, in v. 24: "May his steadfast love remain with Simeon, and may he maintain for him the covenant of Phinehas; may it never be cut off from him and from his seed, as long as the heavens last." The reason for making it so vague was that from about 150 B.C. the priesthood of Phinehas had disappeared, displaced by the upstart Hasmoneans.

## EPIGRAM
50:25-26

> 25With two nations my soul is vexed,
>   and the third is no nation:
> 26Those who live on Mount Seir,
>     and the Philistines,
>   and the foolish people that dwell in Shechem.

In a last numerical proverb Ben Sira denounces three peoples who constitute a threat to the integrity and even survival of Judaism: the Edomites, who menaced Judah on the south; the Philistines, prosperous hellenized neighbors on the west; and the Samaritans, fierce rivals and "heretics," on the north (cf. Jn 4:9). All three were attacked and subjugated by the Hasmonean kings, successors of the Maccabees, within the following century.

## EPILOGUE AND COLOPHON
50:27-29

> 27Instruction in understanding and knowledge
>   I have written in this book,
> Jesus the son of Sirach, son of
>     Eleazar, of Jerusalem
>   who out of his heart poured forth wisdom.
> 28Blessed is he who concerns himself with these things,
>   and he who lays them to heart will become wise.
> 29For if he does them, he will be strong for all things,
>   for the light of the Lord is his path.

It was quite unusual that an ancient Hebrew author should attach his name to his work. Ecclesiastes had used the name Qoheleth, Preacher, but that was clearly a pseudonym. But Ben Sira is enough of a hellenist to sign his name. Its form varies in the texts; most probably it was Jeshua ben

Eleazar ben Sira. "Sira" then must have been the name of his grandfather, a man of some importance. 27, the "book" would be a long scroll, of papyrus or of leather, rolled up on a wooden roller. A copy might be made by anyone who could write, and could afford the material. 28, Ben Sira utters the last of his beatitudes, putting happiness and wisdom in parallel. 29b, his original text has "for the fear of the Lord is life," harking back to chap. 1.

# APPENDICES

## INDIVIDUAL PSALM OF THANKSGIVING
## 51:1-12

**51** I will give thanks to thee, O Lord and King,
and will praise thee as God my Savior.
I give thanks to thy name,
² for thou hast been my protector and helper
and hast delivered my body from destruction
and from the snare of a slanderous tongue,
from lips that utter lies.
Before those who stood by thou wast my helper,
³and didst deliver me,
in greatness of thy mercy and of thy name,
from the gnashings of teeth about to devour me,
from the hand of those who sought my life,
from the many afflictions that I endured,
⁴from choking fire on every side
and from the midst of fire which I did not kindle,
⁵from the depths of the belly of Hades,
from an unclean tongue and lying words—
⁶ the slander of an unrighteous tongue to the king.
My soul drew near to death,
and my life was very near to Hades beneath.
⁷They surrounded me on every side,
and there was no one to help me;

> I looked for the assistance of men,
>    and there was none.
> [8]Then I remembered thy mercy, O Lord,
>    and thy work from of old,
> that thou dost deliver those who wait for thee
>    and dost save them from the hand of their enemies.
> [9]And I sent up my supplication from the earth,
>    and prayed for deliverance from death.
> [10]I appealed to the Lord, the Father of my lord,
>    not to forsake me in the days of affliction,
>    at the time when there is no help against the proud.
> [11]I will praise thy name continually,
>    and will sing praise with thanksgiving.
> My prayer was heard,
> [12]   for thou didst save me from destruction
>    and rescue me from an evil plight.
> Therefore I will give thanks to thee and praise thee,
>    and I will bless the name of the Lord.

Thanksgiving psalms, quite frequent in the Psalter, have a recognizable structure. They include an announcement, a narrative which recalls the psalmist's distress, his prayer for rescue and the Lord's saving intervention, then renewed thanks with reference to bystanders and usually to a sacrifice or vow. Here the announcement is in v. 1; the narrative puts the intervention first (vv. 2-5) then the distress (vv. 6-7) then the prayer (8-10). 11-12 repeat the structure more briefly. The piece is an appendix to the book, still it may be Ben Sira's work. More doubtful in origin is the collective thanksgiving, similar in style to Ps 136, which the Hebrew manuscripts insert between vv. 12 and 13 (see NAB, note). It does not appear in the Greek translation, so was probably not part of Ben Sira's original.

## ACROSTIC: TESTIMONY AND EXHORTATION
51:13-30

> [13]While I was still young, before I went on my travels,
>    I sought wisdom openly in my prayer.

[14]Before the temple I asked for her,
and I will search for her to the last.
[15]From blossom to ripening grape
my heart delighted in her;
my foot entered upon the straight path;
from my youth I followed her steps.
[16]I inclined my ear a little and received her,
and I found for myself much instruction.
[17]I made progress therein;
to him who gives me wisdom I will give glory.
[18]For I resolved to live according to wisdom,
and I was zealous for the good;
and I shall never be put to shame.
[19]My soul grappled with wisdom,
and in my conduct I was strict;
I spread out my hands to the heavens,
and lamented my ignorance of her.
[20]I directed my soul to her,
and through purification I found her.
I gained understanding with her from the first,
therefore I will not be forsaken.
[21]My heart was stirred to seek her,
therefore I have gained a good possession.
[22]The Lord gave me a tongue as my reward,
and I will praise him with it.
[23]Draw near to me, you who are untaught,
and lodge in my school.
[24]Why do you say you are lacking in these things,
and why are your souls very thirsty?
[25]I opened my mouth and said,
Get these things for yourselves without money.
[26]Put your neck under the yoke,
and let your souls receive instruction;
it is to be found close by.
[27]See with your eyes that I have labored little
and found for myself much rest.
[28]Get instruction with a large sum of silver,
and you will gain by it much gold.
[29]May your soul rejoice in his mercy,

and may you not be put to shame when you praise him.
30Do your work before the appointed time,
and in God's time he will give you your reward.

This text is an acrostic poem, beginning its successive verses with the successive letters of the Hebrew alphabet. Fragments of what seems to have been an earlier version of it were found among the Qumran materials (the "Dead Sea scrolls") so probably it was not composed by Ben Sira but by some other sage, who however shared much of Ben Sira's outlook. It was added to the book as an appendix in the course of the editing and expansion described above (Introduction, p. 18). In the first half (vv. 13-22) the author speaks of his personal experience: he personifies Wisdom as a beautiful young maiden whom he desired to woo and to take for his own. By persevering prayer, study and purification he achieved his end—though here too he is careful to specify (v. 17) that it was God's gift. In the second half (23-30) he invites the unwise and untaught to imitate his example. Verse 23, "school" is "house of learning," a technical name for the place where students assembled for instruction in the Law. 24-27 seems to echo Isa 55:1-3. In v. 28 "silver" and "gold" are of course figurative: "labor" and "wisdom."

# FOR FURTHER READING

E. L. Beavin, "Ecclesiasticus," in *Interpreter's One-Volume Commentary on the Bible* (1971), 550-576

D. Cox, *Proverbs, with an Introduction to Sapiential Books,* Wilmington, 1982.

James L. Crenshaw, *Old Testament Wisdom: an Introduction,* Richmond, 1981

A. A. Di Lella, "Conservative and Progressive Theology: Sirach and Wisdom," *Catholic Biblical Quarterly* 28 (1966), 139-154

_____, "The Wisdom of Ben Sira," *Bible Today* 1979, 1954-1961

M. Hengel, *Judaism and Hellenism,* Philadelphia, 1974

C. Kearns, "Sirach", in *A New Catholic Commentary on Holy Scripture,* Camden, 1969

L. G. Perdue, *Wisdom and Cult,* Missoula, 1977

G. von Rad, *Wisdom in Israel,* New York, 1973

W. Roth, "The Lord's Glory Fills Creation...," *Explor* 6(1981) 85-95

J. G. Snaith, *Ecclesiasticus,* Cambridge Bible Commentary, Cambridge, 1974

V. Tcherikover, *Hellenistic Civilization and the Jews,* Philadelphia, 1966

B. Vawter, *Book of Sirach,* Pamphlet Bible Series, 40, 41, New York, 1962

T. H. Weber, "Sirach," in *The Jerome Biblical Commentary* Englewood Cliffs, 1968